200 Light

weekday me

D0245025

hamlyn | **all colour cookbook**

200 Light
weekday meals

An Hachette UK Company
www.hachette.co.uk

First published in Great Britain in 2014 by Hamlyn
a division of Octopus Publishing Group Ltd, Endeavour
House, 189 Shaftesbury Avenue, London, WC2H 8JY
www.octopusbooks.co.uk

ISBN: 978-0-600-62898-9
A CIP catalogue record for this book is available
from the British Library.

Printed and bound in China

10 9 8 7 6 5 4 3 2 1

Both metric and imperial measurements have been given
in all recipes. Use one set of measurements only, and not a
mixture of both.

Standard level spoon measurements are used in all recipes.
1 tablespoon = one 15 ml spoon
1 teaspoon = one 5 ml spoon

Ovens should be preheated to the specified temperature
– if using a fan-assisted oven, follow the manufacturer's
instructions for adjusting the time and temperature.

Fresh herbs should be used unless otherwise stated.

Medium eggs should be used unless otherwise stated.

The Department of Health advises that eggs should not
be consumed raw. This book contains some dishes made
with raw or lightly cooked eggs. It is prudent for vulnerable
people such as pregnant and nusing mothers, invalids,
the elderly, babies and young children to avoid uncooked
or lightly cooked dishes made with eggs. Once prepared,
these dishes should be kept refrigerated and used promptly.

This book includes dishes made with nuts and nut
derivatives. It is advisable for those with known allergic
reactions to nuts and nut derivatives and those who may
be potentially vulnerable to these allergies to avoid dishes
made with nuts and nut oils. It is also prudent to check the
labels of pre-prepared ingredients for the possible inclusion
of nut derivatives.

contents

Introduction

Introduction

This series

The Hamlyn All Colour Light Series is a collection of handy-sized books, each packed with over 200 healthy recipes on a variety of topics and cuisines to suit your needs.

The books are designed to help those people who are trying to lose weight by offering a range of delicious recipes that are low in calories but still high in flavour. The recipes shows the calorie count per portion, so you will know exactly what you are eating. These are recipes for real and delicious food, not ultra-slimming meals, so they will help you maintain your new, healthier eating plan for life. They must be used as part of a balanced diet, with the cakes and sweet dishes eaten only as an occasional treat.

How to use this book

All the recipes in this book are clearly marked with the number of calories (kcal) per serving. The chapters cover different calorie bands: Under 500 calories, under 400 calories, etc.

There are variations of each recipe at the bottom of the page — note the calorie count as they do vary and can sometimes be more than the original recipe.

The figures assume that you are using low-fat versions of dairy products, so be sure to use skimmed milk and low-fat yogurt. They have also been calculated using lean meat, so make sure you trim meat of all visible fat and remove the skin from chicken breasts. Use moderate amounts of oil and butter for cooking and low-fat/low-calorie alternatives when you can.

Don't forget to take note of the number of portions each recipe makes and divide up the quantity of food accordingly, so that you know exactly how many calories you are consuming. Be careful about side dishes and accompaniments as they will add to the calorie content.

Above all, enjoy trying out the new flavours and exciting recipes that this book contains. Rather than dwelling on the thought that you are denying yourself your usual unhealthy treats, think of your new regime as a positive step towards a new you. Not only will you lose weight and feel more confident, but your health will benefit, the condition of your hair and nails will improve, and you will take on a healthy glow.

The risks of obesity

Up to half of women and two-thirds of men are overweight or obese in the developed world today. Being overweight not only can make us unhappy with our appearance, but can also lead to serious health problems, including heart disease, high blood pressure and diabetes.

When someone is obese, it means they are overweight to the point that it could start to seriously threaten their health. In fact, obesity ranks as a close second to smoking as a possible cause of cancer. Obese women are more likely to have complications during and after pregnancy, and people who are overweight or obese are also more likely to suffer from coronary heart disease, gallstones, osteoarthritis, high blood pressure and type 2 diabetes.

How can I tell if I am overweight?

The best way to tell if you are overweight is to work out your body mass index (BMI). If using metric measurements, divide your weight in kilograms (kg) by your height in metres (m) squared. (For example, if you are 1.7 m tall and weigh 70 kg, the calculation would be $70 \div 2.89 = 24.2$.) If using imperial measurements, divide your weight in pounds (lb) by your height in inches (in) squared and

multiply by 703. Then compare the figure to the list below (these figures apply to healthy adults only).

Less than 20	underweight
20–25	healthy
25–30	overweight
Over 30	obese

As we all know by now, one of the major causes of obesity is eating too many calories.

What is a calorie?

Our bodies need energy to stay alive, grow, keep warm and be active. We get the energy we need to survive from the food and drinks we consume – more specifically, from the fat, carbohydrate, protein and alcohol that they contain.

A calorie (cal), as anyone who has ever been on a diet will know, is the unit used to measure how much energy different foods contain. A calorie can be scientifically defined as the energy required to raise the temperature of 1 gram of water from 14.5°C to 15.5°C. A kilocalorie (kcal) is 1,000 calories and it is, in fact, kilocalories that we usually mean when we talk about the calories in different foods.

Different food types contain different numbers of calories. For example, a gram of carbohydrate (starch or sugar) provides 3.75 kcal, protein provides 4 kcal per gram, fat provides 9 kcal per gram and alcohol provides 7 kcal per gram. So, fat is the most concentrated source of energy – weight for weight, it provides just over twice as many calories as either protein or carbohydrate – with alcohol not far behind. The energy content of a food or drink depends on how many grams of carbohydrate, fat, protein and alcohol are present.

How many calories do we need?

The number of calories we need to consume varies from person to person, but your body weight is a clear indication of whether you are eating the right amount. Body weight is simply determined by the number of calories you are eating compared to the number of calories your body is using to maintain itself and needed for physical activity. If you regularly consume more calories than you use up, you will start to gain weight as extra energy is stored in the body as fat.

Based on our relatively inactive modern-day lifestyles, most nutritionists recommend that women should aim to consume around 2,000

calories (kcal) per day, and men an amount of around 2,500. Of course, the amount of energy required depends on your level of activity: the more active you are, the more energy you need to maintain a stable weight.

A healthier lifestyle

To maintain a healthy body weight, we need to expend as much energy as we eat; to lose weight, energy expenditure must therefore exceed intake of calories. So, exercise is a vital tool in the fight to lose weight. Physical activity doesn't just help us control body weight; it also helps to reduce our appetite and is known to have beneficial effects on the heart and blood that help prevent against cardiovascular disease.

Many of us claim we don't enjoy exercise and simply don't have the time to fit it into our hectic schedules, so the easiest way to increase physical activity is by incorporating it into our daily routines, perhaps by walking or cycling instead of driving (particularly for short journeys), taking up more active hobbies such as gardening, and taking small and simple steps, such as using the stairs instead of the lift whenever possible.

As a general guide, adults should aim to undertake at least 30 minutes of moderate-intensity exercise, such as a brisk walk, five times a week. The 30 minutes does not have to be taken all at once: three sessions of 10 minutes are equally beneficial. Children and young people should be encouraged to take

at least 60 minutes of moderate-intensity exercise every day.

Some activities will use up more energy than others. The following list shows some examples of the energy a person weighing 60 kg (132 lb) would expend doing the following activities for 30 minutes:

activity	energy
Ironing	69 kcal
Cleaning	75 kcal
Walking	99 kcal
Golf	129 kcal
Fast walking	150 kcal
Cycling	180 kcal
Aerobics	195 kcal
Swimming	195 kcal
Running	300 kcal
Sprinting	405 kcal

2,000 per day thereafter to maintain her new body weight. Regular exercise will also make a huge difference: the more you can burn, the less you will need to diet.

Improve your diet

For most of us, simply adopting a more balanced diet will reduce our calorie intake and lead to weight loss. Follow these simple recommendations:

Eat more starchy foods, such as bread, potatoes, rice and pasta. Assuming these replace the fattier foods you usually eat, and you don't smother them with oil or butter, this will help reduce the amount of fat and increase the amount of fibre in your diet. As a bonus, try to use wholegrain rice, pasta and flour, as the energy from these foods is released more slowly in the body, making you feel fuller for longer.

Eat more fruit and vegetables, aiming for at least five portions of different fruit and vegetables a day (excluding potatoes). As long as you don't add extra fat to your fruit and vegetables in the form of cream, butter or oil, these changes will help reduce your fat intake and increase the amount of fibre and vitamins you consume.

Eat fewer sugary foods, such as biscuits, cakes and chocolate bars. This will also help reduce your fat intake. If you fancy something sweet, aim for fresh or dried fruit instead.

Reduce the amount of fat in your diet, so you consume fewer calories. Choosing low-fat

Make changes for life

The best way to lose weight is to try to adopt healthier eating habits that you can easily maintain all the time, not just when you are trying to slim down. Aim to lose no more than 1 kg (2 lb) per week to ensure you lose only your fat stores. People who go on crash diets lose lean muscle as well as fat and are much more likely to put the weight back on again soon afterwards.

For a woman, the aim is to reduce her daily calorie intake to around 1,500 kcal while she is trying to lose weight, then settle on around

versions of dairy products, such as skimmed milk and low-fat yogurt, doesn't necessarily mean your food will be tasteless. Low-fat versions are available for most dairy products, including milk, cheese, crème fraîche, yogurt, and even cream and butter.

Choose lean cuts of meat, such as back bacon instead of streaky, and chicken breasts instead of thighs. Trim all visible fat off meat before cooking and avoid frying foods – grill or roast instead. Fish is also naturally low in fat and can make a variety of tempting dishes.

Simple steps to reduce your intake:

Few of us have an iron will, so when you are trying to cut down make it easier on yourself by following these steps:

- Serve small portions to start with. You may feel satisfied when you have finished, but if you are still hungry you can always go back for more.
- Once you have served up your meal, put away any leftover food before you eat. Don't put heaped serving dishes on the table as you will undoubtedly pick, even if you feel satisfied with what you have already eaten.
- Eat slowly and savour your food; then you are more likely to feel full when you have finished. If you rush a meal, you may still feel hungry afterwards.
- Make an effort with your meals. Just because you are cutting down doesn't mean your meals have to be low on taste as well as calories. You will feel more satisfied with a meal you have really enjoyed and will be less likely to look for comfort in a bag of crisps or a bar of chocolate.

- Plan your meals in advance to make sure you have all the ingredients you need. Searching the cupboards when you are hungry is unlikely to result in a healthy, balanced meal.
- Keep healthy and interesting snacks to hand for those moments when you need something to pep you up. You don't need to succumb to a chocolate bar if there are other tempting treats on offer.

WEEKDAY MEALS

When we stop to think about our modern lives, it's easy to see how meals can get pushed into

the background and be made to fit around our other commitments. Time is in such short supply that most of us scarcely have time to eat our meals, let alone plan them, shop for them and cook them. That is why we have included the recipes in this book, which bring together some delicious and nutritious dishes that all the family can enjoy together and that will only take a short time to prepare and cook.

For many, cooking in the week is a bore; it is a 'must-do' activity rather than a 'like-to'. Energy and creativity levels are low, there's very little time and there are other things you need to be getting on with. So we have come up with this book to put the pleasure back into cooking meals midweek. We believe that no matter how little time you have, cooking should be a creative, therapeutic, enjoyable process with an end result you can be proud

of. But we are realistic; we know time is tight; there is paperwork to do after dinner and the house needs cleaning before your guests arrive tomorrow.

Take time to plan healthy balanced meals

Some 'food in a hurry'-style cookery books assume you have an army of helpers in your kitchen and an array of special gadgets and equipment to speed up the prep process. We make no such assumptions. We do however hope that you will take a little time to plan and buy for your dishes because the key to midweek meal success is preparation. Use some of your lunch-hour or some time at the weekend to browse through this book and choose four or five meals that you'd like to serve in the week. Then once you've worked out what ingredients you need, ensure you get everything in stock ready for the beginning of the week. Don't forget internet shopping and home-delivery services – they are designed for busy people and can be arranged for times that suit you and your busy schedule.

Mix it Up

It may seem obvious, but when you are planning your week's meals, try to get a good balance of different foods on your plate each day and through the week. We have planned the recipes in this book to help give you a broad range of nutrient-dense foods across the week, but the key is to mix up your menus

and not always cook the same types of food. We would suggest that you bear the following in mind when you are creating your meal plan:

- Eat fish at least twice a week as it is known to reduce heart disease, is rich in B and D vitamins and contains high levels of Omega 3 which is great for your heart.
- Chicken can be eaten as often as your budget allows, but try to afford organic where possible.
- If you are a red-meat addict, choose lean cuts where possible and cuts which lend themselves to quick cooking. Limit red meat to twice a week.
- Offal is an excellent source of vitamins, copper, iron and zinc, however, as the liver tends to accumulate chemical residues from the animal, limit your intake to once a week.
- Nuts and seeds are nutritional gems. They are low in saturated fats, high in protein and fibre, and are brimming with B vitamins and many useful minerals.
- Eggs are a quick and healthy protein source and low in saturated fat – current thinking is that up to 6 eggs per week is a perfectly healthy addition to your diet.
- Mix up your vegetables as much as your budget allows. Include root and leafy veg and as many different colours as you can. All vegetables contain high levels of vitamin C, many contain important B vitamins and all are abundant in fibre. What's more, when they are cooked lightly and quickly as many are in this book, their goodness is retained

and their benefits are felt all the more.
- Always choose wholegrains as these are good for your heart and keep you fuller for longer.

A well-stocked kitchen

It helps if you keep your kitchen well stocked at all times so you only have to buy the fresh and one-off ingredients each week. For those who keep their cupboards quite lean, this can be a rather time-consuming and possibly expensive exercise initially, but it is worth it to keep costs down thereafter and to reduce time spent shopping each week.

To whizz up a magical meal in minutes, you are going to need some basics in your cupboards. Plain flour and cornflour and a bottle of UHT milk for making emergency sauces, cans of chopped tomatoes chickpeas and beans, passata, tomato paste, strong

form that can be quickly and easily squeezed into the pan when cooking.

Jars of preserved vegetables are a tasty, easy addition to many pastas, salads and rice dishes and can be stored for months, if not years, very successfully as long as they are kept cool. Therefore it would not go amiss to treat yourself to some jars of artichokes, olives and roasted red peppers, and to add the occasional kick to your cooking, keep some capers and anchovies in stock too; you'd be surprised how much these tiny additions add to a meal.

You may not think of yourself as a gardener, but learning to keep a few potted herbs on the windowsill will benefit you no end when it comes to adding quick and easy flavour to a midweek meal. Easy-to-keep herbs include basil, coriander, chives and rosemary. Oregano and thyme can be a little trickier to keep, however these can be bought fresh in bunches and frozen for when you need them. Don't be concerned if the leaves go very dark or black – they will retain their flavour.

The fridge and freezer

Make space in your fridge for some key ingredients that form the basis for many meals: onions, garlic, hard cheese, a good strong parmesan and some natural yoghurt. Keep quartered lemons and limes, ginger and chillies in the freezer, plus nutrient-rich veggies that freeze well such as spinach, peas or sweetcorn. Bacon, chicken and fish fillets and sausages can be separated and frozen

English mustard, a good selection of oils including a basic vegetable oil such as sunflower oil, a good quality olive oil, and some more alternative flavours such as peanut, sesame and walnut. Always have a good quality balsamic vinegar in the cupboard, and for those dishes with an oriental twist, stock up on coconut milk, soy sauce, fish sauce, sweet chilli dipping sauce, hoi sin, plus a selection of your preferred noodles and rice.

Don't be afraid to buy some 'cheat' ingredients for those super-quick meals you're going to prepare; pesto sauces, ready-made pizza bases and Thai curry paste are must haves for busy days, plus remember you can buy garlic, ginger and lemongrass in paste-in small servings ready for easy defrosting, or buy bags of frozen prawns, mussels or mixed seafood for an easy addition to soups, stews and stir fries.

When a loaf of bread is no longer fresh enough to eat in slices, whizz up the loaf in a food processor and freeze the breadcrumbs in small food bags ready for coating your chicken or fish fillets. Remember, too, that bread freezes well and bags of muffins and burger buns kept in the freezer are sure to get good use.

Short cuts

If you do not have a microwave and have forgotten to take meat, poultry or fish out of the freezer, you can speed up the process of defrosting by immersing the wrapped frozen food in a sink of cold water and leaving it for a couple of hours.

Instead of crushing garlic, chop the end off a clove and grate it instead. It saves time washing up the garlic crusher and wastes less of the clove. If the recipe requires a large number of garlic cloves, you can save time by adding garlic paste straight from the tube. The flavour is intense, so take care; you need only a small amount to replace a clove of garlic.

Fresh coriander is a wonderful herb, which adds huge amounts of flavour to all sorts of dishes. Make sure you always have the flavour of 'fresh coriander' by keeping a store of pots or tubes of coriander paste, which preserves the coriander leaves in a mixture of oil and vinegar. Alternatively, freeze a bunch of fresh

coriander in a polythene bag ready to crumble into your cooking. Freezing will blacken the leaves and only marginally reduce the fresh coriander taste.

Fast food that's good for you

Whether you are young or old, a vegetarian or an omnivore, we all need much the same nutrients from the food we eat. Our energy comes from food and fluids, and if we are to get the full and complete range of nutrients that our bodies need we should be consuming carbohydrates, protein, fats, fibre and water as well as a variety of vitamins and minerals. These nutrients not only fuel our bodies, but many of them also actually improve our health and help protect us against diseases. If we eat well, we feel well, our mood is improved, and we can cope better with stress – which can only be a good thing if we're running a busy household.

When you have tried some of the recipes in this book, we sincerely hope you rediscover the joys of midweek cooking. Yes, life is busy, there is always a mountain of jobs that need to be done, but cooking your midweek meal is one job that can be enjoyable, creative and rewarding. So pick a recipe and get cooking! You could find yourself calmer, happier and satisfied in more ways than one!

recipes
under 200
calories

black sesame seeds with prawns

Calories per serving **132**
Serves **4 (with 2 other main dishes)**
Preparation time **10 minutes**
Cooking time **about 10 minutes**

½ tablespoon **black sesame seeds**
1½ tablespoons **sunflower oil**
2–3 **garlic cloves**, finely chopped
250 g (8 oz) **raw prawns**, peeled and deveined
200 g (7 oz) **water chestnuts**, drained and thinly sliced
125 g (4 oz) **mangetout**, trimmed
2 tablespoons **vegetable stock, seafood stock** or **water**
1 tablespoon **light soy sauce**
1 tablespoon **oyster sauce**

Dry-fry the black sesame seeds in a small pan for 1–2 minutes or until they are fragrant, then set them aside.

Heat the oil in a wok or large frying pan and stir-fry the garlic over a medium heat until it is lightly browned.

Add the prawns, water chestnuts and mangetout and stir-fry over a high heat for 1–2 minutes. Add the stock, soy sauce and oyster sauce and stir-fry for another 2–3 minutes or until the prawns open and turn pink. Stir in the fried sesame seeds and serve immediately.

For homemade seafood stock, put 1.8 litres (3 pints) cold water, 1 onion (outer skins removed, root cut off, quartered), 1 carrot (roughly chopped), 3 garlic cloves (unpeeled, lightly bruised), 20 cm (8 inches) lemon grass stalks (bruised, roughly sliced), 2.5 cm (1 inch) piece of fresh root ginger (peeled, finely sliced), 3 whole coriander plants (cleaned, the roots lightly bruised), 30 sun-dried goji berries (optional) and 5 black peppercorns in a large saucepan. Heat over a medium heat to boiling point. Reduce to a low heat and simmer for 10 minutes. During simmering, skim from time to time. Add 250 g (8 oz) fish heads, tails and bones (cleaned) or mixed fish bones and prawn shells, simmering for another 10–15 minutes. Strain the stock into a clean bowl.
Calories per serving 132

peppered beef with salad leaves

Calories per serving **148**
Serves **6**
Preparation time **20 minutes**
Cooking time **4–7 minutes**

2 **thick-cut sirloin steaks**,
   about 500 g (1 lb) in total
3 teaspoons **coloured**
   peppercorns, coarsely
   crushed
coarse salt flakes
200 g (7 oz) **natural yogurt**
1–1½ teaspoons **horseradish**
   sauce (to taste)
1 **garlic clove**, crushed
150 g (5 oz) **mixed green**
   salad leaves
100 g (3½ oz) **button**
   mushrooms, sliced
1 **red onion**, thinly sliced
1 tablespoon **olive oil**
salt and **pepper**

Trim the fat from the steaks and rub the meat with the crushed peppercorns and salt flakes.

Mix together the yogurt, horseradish sauce and garlic and season to taste with salt and pepper. Add the salad leaves, mushrooms and most of the red onion and toss together gently.

Heat the oil in a frying pan, add the steaks and cook over a high heat for 2 minutes until browned. Turn over and cook for 2 minutes for medium rare, 3–4 minutes for medium or 5 minutes for well done.

Spoon the salad leaves into the centre of six serving plates. Thinly slice the steaks and arrange the pieces on top, then garnish with the remaining red onion.

For lemon beef with mustard dressing, trim the steaks and season with salt and a light grinding of black pepper. Make the salad as above, replacing the yogurt with 200 g (7 oz) half-fat crème fraîche and using 2 tablespoons wholegrain mustard instead of the horseradish. Cook the steaks as above, adding the juice of ½ lemon to the frying pan after removing the steaks from the heat. Turn the steaks in the lemon a couple of times, then serve as above. **Calories per serving 219**

mussels in black bean sauce

Calories per serving **129**
Serves **4 as a starter**
Preparation time **15 minutes**
Cooking time **7 minutes**

1 kg (2 lb) **live mussels**
1 tablespoon **groundnut oil**
2 **garlic cloves**, finely sliced
2 tablespoons **black bean sauce**
1 tablespoon **chopped fresh root ginger**
2 tablespoons **Chinese rice wine** or **dry sherry**
1 tablespoon **light soy sauce**
4 tablespoons **water**
handful of **coriander leaves**, roughly chopped

Scrub the mussels thoroughly under cold running water. Pull off the hairy 'beards' and rinse again. Gently tap any open mussels and discard any that don't close.

Heat the oil in a wok over a medium heat. Add the garlic and fry until crisp and golden. Now stir in the black bean sauce, ginger, rice wine and soy sauce. Pour in the water and boil for 1 minute.

Throw in the mussels, cover and simmer over a medium heat for 3–4 minutes, until all the mussels have opened, discarding any that remain closed. Stir in the coriander and serve immediately.

For king prawns with oyster sauce, heat the oil and add all the ingredients for the sauce, replacing the black bean sauce with oyster sauce. Omit the mussels and add 250 g (8 oz) raw peeled king prawns. Simmer for 2–3 minutes until pink all the way through and serve with a scattering of shredded spring onions.
Calories per serving 105

turkey ragout

Calories per serving **190**
Serves **4**
Preparation time **10 minutes**
Cooking time **1 hour
50 minutes**

1 **turkey drumstick**, about
625 g (1¼ lb)
2 **garlic cloves**
15 **baby onions** or **shallots**
3 **carrots**, diagonally sliced
300 ml (½ pint) **red wine**
a few **thyme sprigs**
2 **bay leaves**
2 tablespoons chopped **flat
leaf parsley**
1 teaspoon **port wine jelly**
1 teaspoon **wholegrain
mustard**
salt and **pepper**

Carefully remove the skin from the turkey drumstick and make a few cuts in the flesh. Finely slice 1 of the garlic cloves and push the slivers into the slashes. Crush the remaining garlic clove.

Transfer the drumstick to a large, flameproof casserole or roasting tin with the onions or shallots, carrots, crushed garlic, red wine, thyme and bay leaves. Season well with salt and pepper, cover and place in a preheated oven, 180°C (350°F), Gas Mark 4, for about 1¾ hours or until the turkey is cooked through.

Remove the turkey and vegetables from the casserole and keep hot. Bring the sauce to the boil on the hob, discarding the bay leaves. Add the parsley, port wine jelly and mustard. Boil for 5 minutes, until slightly thickened. Season with salt and pepper. Carve the turkey and serve with the juices in 4 serving bowls.

hot & sour soup

Calories per serving **161**
Serves **4**
Preparation time **10 minutes**
Cooking time **12 minutes**

750 ml (1¼ pints) **vegetable
  or fish stock**
4 dried **kaffir lime leaves**
2.5 cm (1 inch) piece **fresh
  root ginger**, peeled and
  grated
1 **red chilli**, deseeded and
  sliced
1 **lemon grass stalk**, lightly
  bruised
125 g (4 oz) **mushrooms**,
  sliced
100 g (3½ oz) **rice noodles**
75 g (3 oz) **baby spinach**
125 g (4 oz) cooked, peeled
  tiger prawns, or defrosted if
  frozen, rinsed with cold water
  and drained
2 tablespoons **lemon juice**
freshly ground **black pepper**

Put the stock, lime leaves, fresh root ginger, chilli and lemon grass in a large saucepan. Cover and bring to the boil. Add the mushrooms and simmer for 2 minutes. Break the noodles into short lengths, drop into the soup and simmer for 3 minutes.

Add the baby spinach and prawns and simmer for 2 minutes until the prawns are heated through. Add the lemon juice. Remove and discard the lemon grass stalk and season the soup with black pepper before serving.

For hot coconut soup, make up the soup as above, adding just 450 ml (¾ pint) stock and a 400 ml (14 fl oz) can coconut milk, plus 2 teaspoons ready-made Thai red curry paste. Continue as above and serve sprinkled with a little chopped coriander. **Calories per serving 348**

tuna & borlotti bean salad

Calories per serving **190**
Serves **4**
Preparation time **15 minutes,
plus marinating**
Cooking time **3 minutes**

400 g (13 oz) can **borlotti
beans**, drained and rinsed
1 tablespoon **water** (optional)
2 tablespoons **extra virgin
olive oil**
2 **garlic cloves**, crushed
1 **red chilli**, deseeded and
finely chopped
2 **celery sticks**, thinly sliced
½ **red onion**, cut into thin
wedges
200 g (7 oz) can **tuna in olive
oil**, drained and flaked
finely grated **rind** and **juice** of
1 **lemon**
50 g (2 oz) **wild rocket leaves**
salt and **pepper**

Heat the borlotti beans in a saucepan over a medium heat for 3 minutes, adding the measurement water if starting to stick to the base.

Put the oil, garlic and chilli in a large bowl. Stir in the celery, onion and hot beans and season with salt and pepper. Cover and leave to marinate at room temperature for at least 30 minutes and up to 4 hours.

Stir in the tuna and lemon rind and juice. Gently toss in the rocket leaves, taste and adjust the seasoning with extra salt, pepper and lemon juice, if necessary.

For a mixed bean salad, heat the borlotti beans, as above, with a 400 g (13 oz) can drained and rinsed cannellini beans. Leave to marinate with the other salad ingredients as above, but also adding 2 tablespoons roughly chopped flat leaf parsley. After marinating, toss in 50 g (2 oz) lambs' lettuce, season with salt and pepper and serve. **Calories per serving 175**

red pepper & feta rolls with olives

Calories per serving **146 (not including rocket and crusty bread)**
Serves **4**
Preparation time **10 minutes, plus cooling**
Cooking time **10 minutes**

2 **red peppers**, cored, deseeded and quartered lengthways
100 g (3½ oz) **feta cheese**, thinly sliced or crumbled
16 **basil leaves**
16 **black olives**, pitted and halved
15 g (½ oz) **pine nuts**, toasted
1 tablespoon **pesto**
1 tablespoon **fat-free French dressing**

Place the peppers skin-side up on a baking sheet under a high grill and cook for 7–8 minutes until the skins are blackened. Remove the peppers and place them in a plastic bag. Fold over the top to seal and leave to cool for 20 minutes, then remove the skins.

Lay the skinned pepper quarters on a board and layer up the feta, basil leaves, olives and pine nuts on each one.

Carefully roll up the peppers and secure with a cocktail stick. Place two pepper rolls on each serving plate.

Whisk together the pesto and French dressing in a small bowl and drizzle over the pepper rolls. Serve with rocket and crusty bread to mop up the juices, if liked.

For red pepper, ricotta & sun-dried tomato rolls, grill and skin the peppers as above. Mix 5 chopped sun-dried tomatoes (the dry sort, not those in oil) into 100 g (3½ oz) ricotta cheese, also stirring in the basil and pine nuts. Omit the feta and black olives. Season with salt and pepper and use to top the pepper quarters. Roll up and serve as above. **Calories per serving 191**

chilli prawns with garlic & spinach

Calories per serving **124**
Serves **4**
Preparation time **10 minutes**
Cooking time **5 minutes**

2 tablespoons **vegetable oil**
1 **garlic clove**, sliced
1 **red birds eye chilli**,
    deseeded and chopped
300 g (10 oz) **baby spinach**
125 g (4 oz) raw peeled **tiger
    prawns**
3 tablespoons **light soy sauce**
2 teaspoons **caster sugar**
1 tablespoon **Chinese rice
    wine** or **dry sherry**
1 tablespoon **Thai fish sauce
    (nam pla)**
6 tablespoons **water**
Chinese chive flowers or
    chives, to garnish

Heat the oil in a wok over a high heat until the oil starts to shimmer. Add the garlic and chilli and stir-fry for 30 seconds.

Add the spinach and prawns and stir-fry in the oil for 1–2 minutes until the spinach begins to wilt and the prawns are pink and cooked through.

Mix the soy sauce, sugar, rice wine, fish sauce and water together and add to the pan. Quickly stir-fry together for another minute and serve while the spinach still has texture. Garnish with Chinese chive flowers or chives.

For monkfish with lime & spinach, replace the prawns with 250 g (8 oz) monkfish cut into large chunks. Stir-fry the fish with the garlic, chilli and spinach as above, adding in the grated rind and juice of 1 lime with the soy sauce as you remove the stir-fry from the heat. **Calories per serving 135**

prawn & noodle soup

Calories per serving **161**
Serves **4**
Preparation time **10 minutes**
Cooking time **15 minutes**

900 ml (1½ pints) **vegetable**
  or **chicken stock**
2 dried **kaffir lime leaves**
1 **lemon grass stalk**, lightly
  bruised
150 g (5 oz) **dried egg**
  noodles
50 g (2 oz) **frozen peas**
50 g (2 oz) **frozen sweetcorn**
100 g (3½ oz) large **king**
  prawns, cooked, peeled
  and deveined, or defrosted if
  frozen, rinsed with cold water
  and drained
4 **spring onions**, sliced
2 teaspoons **soy sauce**

Put the stock into a saucepan with the lime leaves and lemon grass, bring to the boil, then reduce the heat and simmer for 10 minutes.

Add the noodles to the stock and cook according to the packet instructions. After 2 minutes, add the peas, sweetcorn, prawns, spring onions and soy sauce and cook for 2 more minutes. Remove and discard the lemon grass. Serve the soup in warmed bowls.

For chicken & noodle soup, put the stock, lime leaves and lemon grass into a saucepan, then add 2 boneless, skinless, chicken breasts that have been diced, bring to the boil, then simmer for 10 minutes. Continue as above. **Calories per serving 348**

piperade with pastrami

Calories per serving **186**
Serves **6**
Preparation time **20 minutes**
Cooking time **25 minutes**

6 large **eggs**
thyme sprigs, leaves removed,
    or large pinch of **dried**
    thyme, plus extra sprigs to
    garnish
1 tablespoon **olive oil**
125 g (4 oz) **pastrami**, thinly
    sliced
salt and **pepper**

Sofrito
375 g (12 oz), or 3 small,
    different coloured peppers
1 tablespoon **olive oil**
1 **onion**, finely chopped
2 **garlic cloves**, crushed
500 g (1 lb) **tomatoes**,
    skinned, deseeded and
    chopped

Make the sofrito. Grill or cook the peppers directly in
a gas flame for about 10 minutes, turning them until the
skins have blistered and blackened. Rub the skins from
the flesh and discard. Rinse the peppers under cold
running water. Halve and deseed and cut the flesh
into strips.

Heat the oil in a large frying pan, add the onion
and cook gently for 10 minutes until softened and
transparent. Add the garlic, tomatoes and peppers
and simmer for 5 minutes until any juice has evaporated
from the tomatoes. Set aside until ready to serve.

Beat the eggs with the thyme and salt and pepper in
a bowl. Reheat the sofrito. Heat the oil in a saucepan,
add the eggs, stirring until they are lightly scrambled.
Stir into the reheated sofrito and spoon on to plates.

Arrange slices of pastrami around the eggs and serve
immediately, garnished with a little extra thyme.

For poached egg piperade, make the sofrito as
above. Poach the 6 eggs instead of scrambling them.
Meanwhile, split open 3 English muffins and toast on
both sides. Divide the muffins between 6 plates, then
spoon over the sofrito and sit the eggs over the muffins.
Dust each egg with a tiny pinch of paprika and serve,
omitting the pastrami. **Calories per serving 313**

scallops with lemon & ginger

Calories per serving **143**
Serves **4**
Preparation time **10 minutes**
Cooking time **10 minutes**

15 g (½ oz) **butter**
2 tablespoons **vegetable oil**
8 **scallops**, cut into thick slices
½ bunch of **spring onions**,
   thinly sliced diagonally
½ teaspoon **ground turmeric**
3 tablespoons **lemon juice**
2 tablespoons **Chinese rice**
   wine or **dry sherry**
2 pieces **preserved stem**
   ginger with syrup, chopped
salt and **pepper**

Heat a wok until hot. Add the butter and 1 tablespoon of the oil and heat over a gentle heat until foaming. Add the sliced scallops and stir-fry for 3 minutes, then remove using a slotted spoon and set aside on a plate.

Return the wok to a moderate heat, add the remaining oil and heat until the oil starts to shimmer. Add the spring onions and turmeric and stir-fry for a few seconds. Add the lemon juice and rice wine and bring to a boil, then stir in the stem ginger.

Return the scallops and their juices to the wok and toss until heated through. Season with salt and pepper to taste and serve immediately.

For fennel & carrot salad, to serve with the scallops, use a vegetable peeler to cut 1 fennel bulb and 2 carrots into thin shavings. Toss into a bowl with a handful of coriander leaves, the juice of ½ lemon and ½ teaspoon sesame oil. **Calories per serving 36**

chilli & coriander fish parcels

Calories per serving **127**
Serves **1**
Preparation time **15 minutes,
   plus marinating and
   chilling**
Cooking time **15 minutes**

125 g (4 oz) **cod**, **coley** or
   haddock fillet
2 teaspoons **lemon juice**
1 tablespoon **fresh coriander
   leaves**
1 **garlic clove**
1 **green chilli**, deseeded and
   chopped
¼ teaspoon **sugar**
2 teaspoons **natural yogurt**

Place the fish in a non-metallic dish and sprinkle with the lemon juice. Cover and leave in the refrigerator to marinate for 15–20 minutes.

Put the coriander, garlic and chilli in a food processor or blender and process until the mixture forms a paste. Add the sugar and yogurt and briefly process to blend.

Lay the fish on a sheet of foil. Coat the fish on both sides with the paste. Gather up the foil loosely and turn over at the top to seal. Return to the refrigerator for at least 1 hour.

Place the parcel on a baking tray and bake in a preheated oven, 200°C (400°F), Gas Mark 6, for about 15 minutes until the fish is just cooked.

For spring onion & ginger fish parcels, place the fish fillet on a sheet of foil. Omit the above marinade. Combine 2 thinly sliced spring onions and 1 teaspoon chopped ginger with a pinch of caster sugar and the juice and rind of ½ lime. Rub the mixture all over the fish, then seal and marinate the parcel as above for 30 minutes. Bake as above. **Calories per serving 106**

moroccan baked eggs

Calories per serving **170**
Serves **2**
Preparation time **10 minutes**
Cooking time **25–35 minutes**

½ tablespoon **olive oil**
½ **onion**, chopped
1 **garlic clove**, sliced
½ teaspoon **ras el hanout**
pinch **ground cinnamon**
½ teaspoon **ground coriander**
400 g (13 oz) **cherry tomatoes**
2 tablespoons chopped **coriander leaves**
2 **eggs**
salt and **pepper**

Heat the oil in a frying pan over a medium heat, add the onion and garlic and cook for 6–7 minutes or until softened and lightly golden, stirring occasionally. Stir in the spices and cook for a further 1 minute. Add the tomatoes and season well with salt and pepper, then simmer gently for 8–10 minutes.

Scatter over 3 teaspoons of the coriander, then divide the tomato mixture among 2 individual ovenproof dishes. Break an egg into each dish.

Bake in a preheated oven, 220°C (425°F), Gas Mark 7, for 8–10 minutes until the egg is set but the yolks are still slightly runny. Cook for a further 2–3 minutes if you prefer the eggs to be cooked through. Serve scattered with the remaining coriander.

caponata ratatouille

Calories per serving **90**
Serves **6**
Preparation time **20 minutes**
Cooking time **40 minutes**

750 g (1½ lb) **aubergines**
1 large **onion**
1 tablespoon **olive oil**
3 **celery sticks**, coarsely
  chopped
a little **wine** (optional)
2 large **beef tomatoes**,
  skinned and deseeded
1 teaspoon chopped **thyme**
¼–½ teaspoon **cayenne**
  pepper
2 tablespoons **capers**
handful of **pitted green olives**
4 tablespoons **white wine**
  vinegar
1 tablespoon **sugar**
1–2 tablespoons **cocoa**
  powder (optional)
freshly ground **black pepper**

To garnish
toasted, chopped **almonds**
chopped **parsley**

Cut the aubergines and onion into 1 cm (½ inch) chunks.

Heat the oil in a nonstick frying pan until very hot, add the aubergine and fry for about 15 minutes until very soft. Add a little boiling water to prevent sticking if necessary.

Meanwhile, place the onion and celery in a saucepan with a little water or wine. Cook for 5 minutes until tender but still firm.

Add the tomatoes, thyme, cayenne pepper and aubergine and onions. Cook for 15 minutes, stirring occasionally. Add the capers, olives, wine vinegar, sugar and cocoa powder (if using) and cook for 2–3 minutes.

Season with pepper and serve garnished with almonds and parsley. Serve hot or cold as a side dish, starter or a main dish, with polenta and hot crusty bread, if liked.

For red pepper & potato caponata, omit the aubergines, thyme and cocoa powder. Grill and skin 2 red and 2 yellow peppers, following the method on page 32. Cook the onions and celery as above, then follow the remainder of the recipe, adding the skinned peppers and 500 g (1 lb) cooked and halved new potatoes instead of the aubergines.
Calories per serving 169

seafood with chillies

Calories per serving **174**
Serves **4**
Preparation time **5 minutes**
Cooking time **about**
10 minutes

1 ½ tablespoons **sunflower oil**
3–4 **garlic cloves**, finely
    chopped
125 g (4 oz) **red pepper**,
    deseeded and cut into bite-
    sized pieces
1 **small onion**, cut into eighths
1 **carrot**, cut into matchsticks
450 g (14½ oz) **prepared
    mixed seafood**, such as
    prawns, squid, small scallops
2.5 cm (1 inch) piece of **fresh
    root ginger**, peeled and
    finely grated
2 tablespoons **vegetable** or
    **seafood stock (see
    page 20)**
1 tablespoon **oyster sauce**
½ tablespoon **light soy sauce**
1 **long red chilli**, stemmed,
    deseeded and sliced
    diagonally
1–2 **spring onions**, finely
    sliced

Heat the oil in a nonstick wok or frying pan and stir-fry the garlic over medium heat until it is lightly browned.

Add the red pepper, onion and carrot and stir-fry for 2 minutes.

Add all the seafood together with the ginger, stock, oyster sauce and soy sauce and stir-fry for 2–3 minutes or until the prawns turn pink and all the seafood is cooked.

Add the chilli and spring onions and mix well together. Spoon on to a serving plate and serve immediately, with rice, if liked.

For seafood with pineapple sweet chilli, stir-fry the red pepper, onion and carrot after the garlic has lightly browned. Add all the seafood, ginger, stock, oyster sauce and 2–3 tablespoons pineapple-flavoured sweet chilli sauce (or plain if the flavoured version is unavailable). Omit the spring onion and add a handful of Thai basil leaves with the chilli, lightly toss together for a minute to combine before serving. **Calories per serving 209**

vietnamese beef pho

Calories per serving **158**
Serves **6**
Preparation time **15 minutes**
Cooking time **about 45
   minutes**

1 teaspoon **sunflower oil**
1 teaspoon **Szechuan
   peppercorns**, roughly
   crushed
1 **lemon grass stem**, sliced
1 **cinnamon stick**, broken into
   pieces
2 **star anise**
4 cm (1½ inch) piece of **fresh
   root ginger**, peeled, sliced
small bunch of **coriander**
1.5 litres (2½ pints) **beef
   stock**
1 tablespoon **fish sauce**
juice of **1 lime**
100 g (3½ oz) **fine rice
   noodles**
250 g (8 oz) **rump** or **flash-fry
   beef steak**, fat trimmed,
   meat thinly sliced
100 g (3½ oz) **bean sprouts**,
   rinsed
4 **spring onions**, thinly sliced
1 large **mild red chilli**, thinly
   sliced

Heat the oil in a saucepan, add the peppercorns, lemon grass, cinnamon, star anise and ginger and cook for 1 minute to release their flavours. Cut the stems from the coriander and add the stems to the pan with the stock. Bring to the boil, stirring, then cover and simmer for 40 minutes.

Strain the stock and return to the pan. Stir in the fish sauce and lime juice. Meanwhile, cook the noodles in a pan of boiling water as directed on the pack, then drain and divide between 6 small bowls. Add the steak to the soup and cook for 1–2 minutes. Divide the bean sprouts, spring onions and chilli between the bowls, then ladle the soup on top and finish with the remaining coriander leaves, torn into pieces.

For Vietnamese prawn soup, make up the flavoured broth as above, using 1.5 litres (2½ pints) chicken or vegetable stock and 2 kaffir lime leaves instead of the cinnamon. Simmer for 40 minutes, then drain and finish as above, adding 200 g (7 oz) raw peeled prawns and 150 g (5 oz) sliced button mushrooms instead of the steak, cook for 4–5 minutes until the prawns are pink. Finish with bean sprouts, spring onions and chilli as above. **Calories per serving 135**

recipes
under 300
calories

seafood & vegetable stir-fry

Calories per serving **220**
Serves **4**
Preparation time **18 minutes**
Cooking time **10 minutes**

250 g (8 oz) **live mussels**
250 g (8 oz) **water chestnuts**, peeled and thickly sliced
1 tablespoon **caster sugar**
½ teaspoon **black pepper**
2 tablespoons **vegetable oil**
1 **sweet white onion**, sliced
125 g (4 oz) raw peeled **tiger prawns**
4 **spring onions**, trimmed and diagonally sliced
½ teaspoon **crushed chilli flakes**, plus extra to garnish
125 g (4 oz) **sugar snap peas**, trimmed and diagonally halved
125 g (4 oz) **bean sprouts**
3 tablespoons **light soy sauce**
2 tablespoons **yellow bean sauce**
2 tablespoons **Chinese rice wine** or **dry sherry**
chervil sprigs, to garnish

Scrub the mussels thoroughly under cold running water. Pull off the hairy 'beards' and rinse again. Gently tap any open mussels and discard any that do not close.

Sprinkle the water chestnuts with the sugar and pepper and set aside.

Heat the oil in a wok over a high heat until the oil starts to shimmer. Add the onion and mussels and stir-fry quickly for 1 minute. Put a lid on the wok and cook for 3–4 minutes or until the mussels have opened. Discard any mussels that remain closed.

Add the water chestnuts, prawns, spring onions, chilli flakes, sugar snaps and bean sprouts to the wok and stir-fry for 1–2 minutes or until the prawns have turned pink and are cooked through.

Mix together the soy sauce, yellow bean sauce and rice wine and pour over the ingredients in the wok. Stir-fry for a further 1–2 minutes until hot. Garnish with crushed chilli flakes and chervil sprigs. Serve with rice, if liked.

For quick mixed seafood stir-fry, replace the live mussels and raw prawns with 250 g (8 oz) mixed cooked seafood, now available in most supermarkets. Cook the onions as above, then add the mixed seafood to the wok at the same time as the sauce ingredients. Complete the recipe as above.
Calories per serving 232

minestrone

Calories per serving **260**
Serves **4**
Preparation time **5 minutes**
Cooking time **23 minutes**

2 tablespoons **olive oil**
1 **onion**, chopped
1 **garlic clove**, crushed
2 **celery sticks**, chopped
1 **leek**, finely sliced
1 **carrot**, chopped
400 g (13 oz) can **chopped tomatoes**
600 ml (1 pint) **chicken** or **vegetable stock** (see pages 10 and 13)
1 **courgette**, diced
½ small **cabbage**, shredded
1 **bay leaf**
75 g (3 oz) **canned haricot beans**
75 g (3 oz) **dried spaghetti**, broken into small pieces, or small **pasta shapes**
1 tablespoon chopped **flat leaf parsley**
salt and **pepper**
grated **Parmesan cheese**, to serve

Heat the oil in a large saucepan. Add the onion, garlic, celery, leek and carrot and cook over a medium heat, stirring occasionally, for 5 minutes. Add the tomatoes, stock, courgette, cabbage, bay leaf and haricot beans. Bring to the boil, lower the heat and simmer for 10 minutes.

Add the pasta and season to taste. Stir well and cook for a further 8 minutes. Keep stirring because the soup may stick to the base of the pan. Just before serving, add the parsley and stir well. Ladle into individual bowls and serve with grated Parmesan.

For minestrone with rocket & basil pesto, make up the soup as above, then ladle into bowls. Top with spoonfuls of pesto made by finely chopping 25 g (1 oz) rocket leaves and 25 g (1 oz) basil leaves, 1 garlic clove and 25 g (1 oz) pine nuts. Mix with 2 tablespoons freshly grated Parmesan, a little salt and pepper and 60 ml (2 fl oz) olive oil. Alternatively, put all the pesto ingredients into a liquidizer or food processor and whiz together. (Use only half the quantity the recipe makes to maintain the 350 calorie serving.) **Calories per serving 350**

beef in black bean sauce

Calories per serving **294**
Serves **4**
Preparation time **10 minutes**
Cooking time **10 minutes**

3 tablespoons **groundnut oil**
500 g (1 lb) **lean beef**, cut
    into thin slices
1 **red pepper**, cored,
    deseeded and cut into strips
6 **baby sweetcorn**, cut in half
    lengthways
1 **green chilli**, deseeded and
    cut into strips
3 **shallots**, cut into thin
    wedges
2 tablespoons **black bean
    sauce**
4 tablespoons **water**
1 teaspoon **cornflour** mixed
    to a paste with 1 tablespoon
    water
salt

Heat 1 tablespoon of the oil in a wok over a high heat until the oil starts to shimmer. Add half the beef, season with salt and stir-fry for 2 minutes. When it begins to colour, lift the beef on to a plate using a slotted spoon. Heat another 1 tablespoon of the oil and stir-fry the rest of the beef in the same way.

Return the wok to the heat and wipe it clean with kitchen paper. Heat the remaining oil and tip in the pepper, sweetcorn, chilli and shallots. Stir-fry for 2 minutes before adding the black bean sauce, the measurement water and the cornflour paste. Bring to the boil, return the beef to the wok and stir-fry until the sauce thickens and coats the stir-fry in a velvety glaze. Serve with rice, if liked.

For king prawns with spring onions & black bean sauce, replace the beef with 250 g (8 oz) raw peeled king prawns. Replace the sweetcorn, green chilli and shallots with 75 g (3 oz) bean sprouts, 1 red chilli and 3 spring onions cut into 1 cm (½ inch) pieces, and cook as above. **Calories per serving 171**

pork with broccoli & mushrooms

Calories per serving **286**
Serves **4**
Preparation time **10 minutes**
Cooking time **10 minutes**

1 tablespoon **sesame seeds**
3 tablespoons **groundnut oil**
400 g (13 oz) **lean pork**,
  sliced into thin strips
250 g (8 oz) small **broccoli**
  florets
150 g (5 oz) **shiitake**
  mushrooms, trimmed and
  halved, if large
3 **baby leeks**, trimmed,
  cleaned and thinly sliced
3 tablespoons **Chinese rice**
  wine or **dry sherry**
3 tablespoons **oyster sauce**
2 tablespoons **malt vinegar**
1 teaspoon **caster sugar**
1 teaspoon **clear honey**
½ teaspoon **sesame oil**
1 **red chilli**, thinly sliced

Fry the sesame seeds in a dry wok over a medium heat, stirring until golden. Set aside.

Heat half the oil in a wok over a high heat until the oil starts to shimmer. Add half the pork and stir-fry for 2 minutes until golden. Remove the pork using a slotted spoon and set aside. Heat the remaining oil and stir-fry the rest of the pork in the same way, then return the first batch of pork to the wok.

Add the broccoli, mushrooms and leeks and stir-fry for 2 minutes. Add the rice wine, oyster sauce, malt vinegar, sugar and honey and cook for 1 more minute. Remove from the heat, stir in the toasted sesame seeds, sesame oil and chilli, and serve.

For spring onion rice, to serve with the pork, heat 1 tablespoon groundnut oil in a wok over a high heat. Add 4 sliced spring onions and give them a quick stir, then tip in 250 g (8 oz) cold cooked rice. Stir until heated through, then add ½ teaspoon sesame oil and 1 tablespoon light soy sauce. Stir well and serve. **Calories per serving 124**

warm scallop salad

Calories per serving **257**
Serves **4**
Preparation time **10 minutes**
Cooking time **3 minutes**

250 g (8 oz) **wild
strawberries**, hulled
2 tablespoons **balsamic
vinegar**
1 tablespoon **lemon juice**,
plus juice of 1 **lemon**
50 ml (2 fl oz) **olive oil**
12 **king scallops**, without
corals, cut into 3 slices
250 g (8 oz) **mixed salad
leaves**
salt and **black pepper**

To garnish
1 tablespoon **olive oil**
3 **leeks**, cut into matchstick-
thin strips
20 **wild strawberries** or
8 **larger strawberries**, sliced

Put the strawberries, vinegar, 1 tablespoon lemon juice
and oil in a food processor or blender and process until
smooth. Pass through a fine sieve or muslin cloth to
remove the pips and set aside.

Season the scallops with salt and pepper and the
remaining lemon juice.

Prepare the garnish. Heat the oil in a nonstick frying
pan, add the leeks and cook over a high heat, stirring,
for 1 minute, or until golden brown. Remove and set
aside.

Add the scallop slices to the pan and cook for
20–30 seconds on each side. Divide the salad leaves
into quarters and pile in the centre of individual serving
plates. Arrange the scallop slices over the salad.

Heat the strawberry mixture gently in a small saucepan
for 20–30 seconds, then pour over the scallops and
salad leaves. Scatter over the leeks and garnish with
the strawberries. Sprinkle with a little pepper and serve.

For scallops with soy & honey dressing, whisk
together 2 tablespoons extra virgin olive oil, 1 teaspoon
sesame oil, 1 tablespoon light soy sauce, 2 teaspoons
balsamic vinegar, 1 teaspoon clear honey and pepper
to taste in a bowl. Cook the scallops as above (omitting
the leeks) and arrange over the salad. Heat the dressing
gently as above, then pour over the scallops and salad
leaves. **Calories per serving 173**

bean, kabanos & pepper salad

Calories per serving **250 (not including walnut bread)**
Serves **4**
Preparation time **10 minutes, plus cooling**
Cooking time **20 minutes**

3 **red peppers**, cored and deseeded
1 tablespoon **olive oil**
1 **onion**, sliced
75 g (3 oz) **kabanos sausage**, thinly sliced
2 x 410 g (13½ oz) cans **butter** or **flageolet beans**, rinsed and drained
1 tablespoon **balsamic vinegar**
1 **red chilli**, deseeded and sliced
2 tablespoons chopped **fresh coriander**

Put the peppers on a baking sheet, skin side up, and cook under a preheated hot grill for 8—10 minutes until the skins are blackened. Cover with damp kitchen paper. When the peppers are cool enough to handle, remove the skins and slice the flesh.

Heat the oil in a nonstick frying pan, add the onion and fry for 5—6 minutes until soft. Add the kabanos sausage and fry for 1—2 minutes until crisp.

Mix together the beans and balsamic vinegar, then add the onion and kabanos mixture and the peppers and chilli. Serve the salad with walnut bread, if liked.

For bean, pepper & olive salad with haloumi, omit the kabanos sausage and mix 50 g (2 oz) halved pitted black olives with the beans. Slice and grill 75 g (3 oz) haloumi. Divide the salad among bowls and top with the haloumi. **Calories per serving 248**

steamed fish with preserved plums

Calories per serving **259**
Serves **4**
Preparation time **30 minutes**
Cooking time **20 minutes**

1 kg (2 lb) **whole fish** (such as
pomfret, plaice, snapper or
sea bass), cleaned, scaled (if
necessary), gutted, scored
3–4 times with a sharp knife
3.5 cm (1½ inch) piece of
fresh root ginger, peeled,
finely shredded
50 g (2 oz) **button
mushrooms**, wiped, thinly
sliced
50 g (2 oz) **smoked bacon**,
cut into thin strips
4 **spring onions**, cut into
2.5 cm (1 inch) lengths
2 small **preserved plums**,
lightly bruised
2 tablespoons **light soy sauce**
pinch of **ground white pepper**

To garnish
coriander leaves
a few slices of **red chilli**

Place the fish on a deep plate slightly larger than the
fish. Use a plate that will fit on the rack of a traditional
bamboo steamer basket or on a steamer rack inside
a wok. Sprinkle the fish with the ginger, mushrooms,
bacon, spring onions, preserved plums, soy sauce
and pepper.

Fill a wok or steamer pan with water, cover and bring to
a rolling boil on a high heat. Set the rack or basket over
the boiling water. Cover and steam for 15–20 minutes
(depending on the variety and size of the fish) or until
a skewer will slide easily into the fish.

Remove the fish from the steamer and place on
a warm serving plate. Garnish with coriander leaves
and chilli slices, and serve with jasmine rice, if liked.

For steamed fish with ginger & spring onions, omit
the mushrooms, smoked bacon and preserved plums.
Add 1 tablespoon sunflower oil and 1 tablespoon
sesame oil, and increase the amount of light soy sauce
to 2–3 tablespoons. Drizzle these on top of the fish
with the ginger and spring onions, and steam as above.
Calories per serving 263

italian broccoli & egg salad

Calories per serving **203**
Serves **4**
Preparation time **10 minutes**
Cooking time **8 minutes**

300 g (10 oz) **broccoli**
2 small **leeks**, about 300 g
  (10 oz) in total, trimmed, slit
  and well rinsed
4 tablespoons **lemon juice**
2 tablespoons **olive oil**
2 teaspoons **clear honey**
1 tablespoon **capers**, well
  drained
2 tablespoons chopped
  tarragon, plus extra sprigs
  to garnish
4 hard-boiled **eggs**
salt and **pepper**

Cut the broccoli into florets and thickly slice the stems and the leeks. Put the broccoli in the top of a steamer, cook for 3 minutes, add the leeks and cook for another 2 minutes.

Mix together the lemon juice, oil, honey, capers and tarragon in a salad bowl and season to taste.

Shell and roughly chop the eggs.

Add the broccoli and leeks to the dressing, toss together and sprinkle with the chopped eggs. Garnish with tarragon sprigs and serve warm with extra thickly sliced wholemeal bread, if liked.

For broccoli, cauliflower & egg salad, use 150 g (5 oz) broccoli and 150 g (5 oz) cauliflower instead of 300 g (10 oz) broccoli. Cut the cauliflower into small florets and steam with the broccoli. Serve with a blue cheese dressing made by mixing together 75 g (3 oz) blue cheese, 6 chopped sun-dried tomatoes and 3 tablespoons balsamic vinegar. **Calories per serving 312**

baked cod with tomatoes & olives

Calories per serving **239**
Serves **4**
Preparation time **5 minutes**
Cooking time **15 minutes**

250 g (8 oz) **cherry tomatoes**, halved
100 g (3½ oz) **pitted black olives**
2 tablespoons **capers**
4 **thyme sprigs**, plus extra to garnish
4 **cod fillets**, about 175 g (6 oz) each
2 tablespoons **extra virgin olive oil**
2 tablespoons **balsamic vinegar**
salt and **black pepper**

Combine the tomatoes, olives, capers and thyme sprigs in a roasting tin. Nestle the cod fillets in the pan, drizzle over the oil and balsamic vinegar and season to taste with salt and pepper.

Bake in a preheated oven, 200°C (400°F), Gas Mark 6, for 15 minutes.

Transfer the fish, tomatoes and olives to warmed plates. Spoon the pan juices over the fish. Serve immediately with a mixed green leaf salad, if liked.

For steamed cod with lemon, arrange a cod fillet on each of 4 x 30 cm (12 inch) squares of foil. Top each with ½ teaspoon grated lemon rind, a squeeze of lemon juice, 1 tablespoon extra virgin olive oil and salt and pepper to taste. Fold the edges of the foil together to form parcels, transfer to a baking sheet and cook in a preheated oven, 200°C (400°F), Gas Mark 6, for 15 minutes. Remove and leave to rest for 5 minutes. Open the parcels and serve sprinkled with chopped parsley. **Calories per serving 253**

pork with savoy cabbage

Calories per serving **227**
Serves **4**
Preparation time **15 minutes**
Cooking time **40 minutes**

1 tablespoon **sesame seeds**
2 **garlic cloves**, very finely
sliced
3 **spring onions**, diagonally
sliced into 1.5 cm (¾ inch)
pieces
½ teaspoon **cayenne pepper**
300 g (10 oz) **pork loin**, cut
into thick strips
2 tablespoons **olive oil**
2 teaspoons **sesame oil**
2 tablespoons **soy sauce**
2 teaspoons **clear honey**
400 g (13 oz) **Savoy
cabbage**, cut into strips

Heat a dry heavy-based frying pan until hot, add the sesame seeds and cook, shaking constantly, for 1–2 minutes until golden brown and aromatic. Remove to a cool plate and set aside.

Combine the garlic, spring onions and cayenne pepper in a bowl. Add the pork and mix well.

Heat the oils in a frying pan, add the pork in 3 batches, and stir-fry over a high heat for 5 minutes on each side, or until golden and cooked through. Remove from the pan with a slotted spoon.

Add the soy sauce, honey and cabbage to the pan and toss to mix. Cover and cook over a medium heat for 5–6 minutes.

Return the pork to the pan, add the sesame seeds and toss well. Serve immediately.

For orange & mustard seed rice to serve with the pork, put 225 g (8 oz) jasmine rice in a saucepan and add 450 ml (16 fl oz) cold water and ½ teaspoon salt. Bring to the boil, then reduce the heat, cover with a tight-fitting lid and simmer over a very low heat for 12 minutes. Meanwhile, melt 2 teaspoons butter in a small saucepan, add 1 tablespoon mustard seeds and grated rind of 1 orange and cook gently, stirring, for 2–3 minutes until the mustard seeds turn golden. Remove the rice from the heat, pour in the mustard seed mixture and replace the lid. Leave to stand for 10 minutes, then stir well and serve. **Calories per serving 269**

smoked salmon cones

Calories per serving **270**
Serves **4**
Preparation time **15 minutes**

2 **small cucumbers**, halved
lengthways, deseeded and
cut into thin strips
1 teaspoon prepared **English
mustard**
1 tablespoon **white wine
vinegar**
½ teaspoon **caster sugar**
1 tablespoon finely chopped
dill
2 **flour tortillas**
4 tablespoons **crème fraîche**
125 g (4 oz) **smoked salmon
trimmings**, any larger pieces
cut into wide strips
salt and **pepper**

Put the cucumber strips in a shallow glass or ceramic
bowl. In a small bowl, mix together the mustard, vinegar,
sugar and dill. Season well with salt and pepper, then
pour over the cucumbers. Leave to stand for 5 minutes.

Cut the tortillas in half and lay on a board or work
surface. Spread 1 tablespoon crème fraîche over each
tortilla half.

Divide the smoked salmon pieces between the tortillas
and top with the cucumber mixture. Add a little salt and
pepper, if liked, and roll up each tortilla to form a cone
around the filling. Secure each cone with a cocktail
stick, if liked.

For chicken & mango cones, put 125 g (4 oz) diced,
cooked chicken breast meat, 1 large peeled, stoned
and diced mango and 1 tablespoon chopped coriander
leaves in a bowl. Add 4 tablespoons mayonnaise, a
squeeze of lime juice, and salt and pepper to taste.
Toss gently to combine, then divide between the tortilla
halves and roll up, as above. **Calories per serving 310**

duck, pear & pomegranate salad

Calories per serving **276 (not including molasses)**
Serves **4**
Preparation time **15 minutes**
Cooking time **15–20 minutes**

2 large, lean **duck breasts**
2 **Comice pears**, cored and diced
125 g (4 oz) **mixed leaf and herb salad**
50 g (2 oz) **walnut pieces**
seeds from 1 **pomegranate**

Dressing
2 teaspoons **lime juice**
2 teaspoons **raspberry vinegar**
2 teaspoons **pomegranate molasses** (optional – see right for homemade)
2 tablespoons **walnut oil**
salt and **pepper**

Remove any excess fat from the duck breasts and score the surface using a sharp knife. Heat a ridged griddle pan until hot, then add the duck breasts, skin side down, and cook for 8–10 minutes. Turn them over and cook for a further 5–10 minutes or until cooked to the pinkness desired. Remove from the pan, cover with foil and leave to rest.

Mix together the pears and leaf salad in a bowl. Arrange on serving plates and scatter with the walnut pieces.

Whisk together all the dressing ingredients in a bowl and season to taste. Drizzle over the salad.

Slice the duck breasts and arrange on the salad. Scatter over the pomegranate seeds and serve immediately.

For homemade pomegranate molasses, juice 2 large pomegranates with a citrus press or remove the seeds and pulse in a food processor or blender. Pour the juice into a small saucepan, add 1 tablespoon sugar and stir until the sugar dissolves. Bring to the boil, then reduce the heat and simmer rapidly until reduced to a thick, sticky molasses. Cool and store in an airtight bottle in the refrigerator for up to 2 weeks.
Calories per serving 319

white bean soup provençal

Calories per serving **200 (not including crusty bread)**
Serves **6**
Preparation time **15 minutes, plus soaking**
Cooking time **1¼–1¾ hours**

3 tablespoons **olive oil**
2 **garlic cloves**, crushed
1 small **red pepper**, cored, deseeded and chopped
1 **onion**, finely chopped
250 g (8 oz) **tomatoes**, finely chopped
1 teaspoon finely chopped **thyme**
400 g (14 oz) **dried haricot** or **cannellini beans**, soaked overnight in cold water, rinsed and drained
600 ml (1 pint) **water**
600 ml (1 pint) **vegetable stock**
2 tablespoons finely chopped **flat leaf parsley**
salt and **pepper**

Heat the oil in a large heavy-based saucepan, add the garlic, red pepper and onion and cook over a medium heat for 5 minutes or until softened.

Add the tomatoes and thyme and cook for 1 minute. Add the beans and pour in the measurement water and stock. Bring to the boil, then reduce the heat, cover and simmer for 1–1½ hours until the beans are tender (you may need to allow for a longer cooking time, depending on how old the beans are).

Sprinkle in the parsley and season with salt and pepper. Serve immediately in warm soup bowls with fresh, crusty bread.

For Spanish white bean soup, add 100 g (3½ oz) diced chorizo sausage when frying the onions, garlic and red pepper. Stir in 1 teaspoon pimentón (Spanish smoked paprika) or 1 teaspoon mild chilli powder. Cook for 1 minute until fragrant, then add the tomatoes and continue the recipe as above.
Calories per serving 325

sweet & sour monkfish & prawns

Calories per serving **217**
Serves **4**
Preparation time **10 minutes**
Cooking time **7 minutes**

300 g (10 oz) **monkfish tail**, cut into chunks
200 g (7 oz) raw peeled **tiger prawns**
2 tablespoons **groundnut oil**
2.5 cm (1 inch) piece of **fresh root ginger**, peeled and finely grated
200 g (7 oz) **carrots**, cut into matchsticks
200 g (7 oz) **sugar snap peas**, halved
4 **spring onions**, thinly sliced
salt and **black pepper**

Sweet and sour sauce
150 ml (5 fl oz) **fish** or **vegetable stock**
2½ tablespoons **light soy sauce**
2 teaspoons **tomato purée**
1 tablespoon **cider vinegar**
2 teaspoons **caster sugar**
2 teaspoons **cornflour**
½ teaspoon **salt**

Combine all the ingredients for the sauce. Season the monkfish and prawns with salt and pepper.

Heat the oil in a wok over a high heat until the oil starts to shimmer. Add the fish and prawns and cook for 2 minutes, carefully turning the fish occasionally, then tip in the ginger, carrots, sugar snaps and spring onions.

Fry for 30 seconds, then add the sauce and bring to the boil. Turn down the heat and simmer for 2–3 minutes until the vegetables are just tender and the fish is cooked through. Serve immediately.

For aromatic monkfish & prawns, cook the fish as above up to the stage where you would have added the sweet and sour sauce. Omit this and instead stir-fry for a further 2 minutes, then remove from the heat and toss in a handful each of torn coriander and mint and the juice of 1 lime. **Calories per serving 185**

butternut squash & ricotta frittata

Calories per serving **248**
Serves **6**
Preparation time **10 minutes**
Cooking time **25–30 minutes**

1 tablespoon **extra virgin
    rapeseed oil**
1 **red onion**, thinly sliced
450 g (14½ oz) peeled
    butternut squash, diced
8 **eggs**
1 tablespoon chopped **thyme**
2 tablespoons chopped **sage**
125 g (4 oz) **ricotta cheese**
salt and **pepper**

Heat the oil in a large, deep frying pan with an ovenproof handle over a medium-low heat, add the onion and butternut squash, then cover loosely and cook gently, stirring frequently, for 18–20 minutes or until softened and golden.

Lightly beat the eggs, thyme, sage and ricotta in a jug, then season well with salt and pepper and pour over the butternut squash.

Cook for a further 2–3 minutes until the egg is almost set, stirring occasionally with a heat-resistant rubber spatula to prevent the base from burning.

Slide the pan under a preheated grill, keeping the handle away from the heat, and grill for 3–4 minutes or until the egg is set and the frittata is golden. Slice into 6 wedges and serve hot.

beef & barley brö

Calories per serving **209**
Serves **6**
Preparation time **20 minutes**
Cooking time **2 hours**

25 g (1 oz) **butter**
250 g (8 oz) **braising beef**, fat
  trimmed away and meat cut
  into small cubes
1 large **onion**, finely chopped
200 g (7 oz) **swede**, diced
150 g (5 oz) **carrot**, diced
100 g (3½ oz) **pearl barley**
2 litres (3½ pints) **beef stock**
2 teaspoons **dry English
  mustard** (optional)
salt and **pepper**
chopped **parsley**, to garnish

Heat the butter in a large saucepan, add the beef
and onion and fry for 5 minutes, stirring, until the
beef is browned and the onion just beginning to colour.

Stir in the diced vegetables, pearl barley, stock and
mustard, if using. Season with salt and pepper and
bring to the boil. Cover and simmer for 1¾ hours,
stirring occasionally until the meat and vegetables are
very tender. Taste and adjust the seasoning if needed.
Ladle the soup into bowls and sprinkle with a little
chopped parsley.

For lamb & barley hotchpot, substitute the beef for
250 g (8 oz) diced lamb fillet and fry with the onion as
above. Add the sliced white part of 1 leek, 175 g (6 oz)
each of diced swede, carrot and potato, then mix in
50 g (2 oz) pearl barley, 2 litres (3½ pints) lamb stock,
2–3 sprigs of rosemary and salt and pepper. Bring to
the boil, then cover and simmer for 1¾ hours. Discard
the rosemary, add the remaining thinly sliced green leek
and cook for 10 minutes. Ladle into bowls and sprinkle
with a little extra chopped rosemary to serve.
Calories per serving 209

baked fish with lemon grass

Calories per serving **284**
Serves **4**
Preparation time **10 minutes**
Cooking time **20–25 minutes**

1 kg (2 lb) **whole fish** (such as
mackerel, St Peter fish, sea
bream, red snapper or grey
mullet), cleaned and scaled
(if necessary), gutted, scored
3–4 times with a sharp knife
4 x 12 cm (5 inch) stalks
lemon grass, cut diagonally
into 2.5 cm (1 inch) lengths
2 **carrots**, cut into matchsticks
4 tablespoons **light soy sauce**
2 tablespoons **lime juice**
1 **red chilli**, finely chopped

To garnish
coriander leaves
a few slices of **red chilli**
a few slices of **lemon**, to serve

Place the fish in a baking dish and sprinkle with the
lemon grass, carrots, 1½ tablespoons of the light soy
sauce and the lime juice.

Cover the baking dish with foil and bake in a preheated
oven, 180°C (350°F), Gas Mark 4, for 20–25 minutes
or until a skewer will slide easily into the flesh and come
out clean. Place the fish on a warm serving plate and
spoon over the sauce. Garnish with coriander leaves
and chilli and serve with the lemon slices.

Spoon the remaining light soy sauce into a small bowl
with the chilli and serve separately.

Serve with other dishes, with boiled rice or on its own
as a light meal with stir-fried or steamed vegetables.

For coley fillets with lemon grass, replace the whole
fish with 4 x 250 g (8 oz) coley fillets, removing any fine
bones. Sprinkle as above and bake for 15–17 minutes
or until the fish is cooked. Garnish with finely chopped
red chilli and serve as above. **Calories per serving 268**

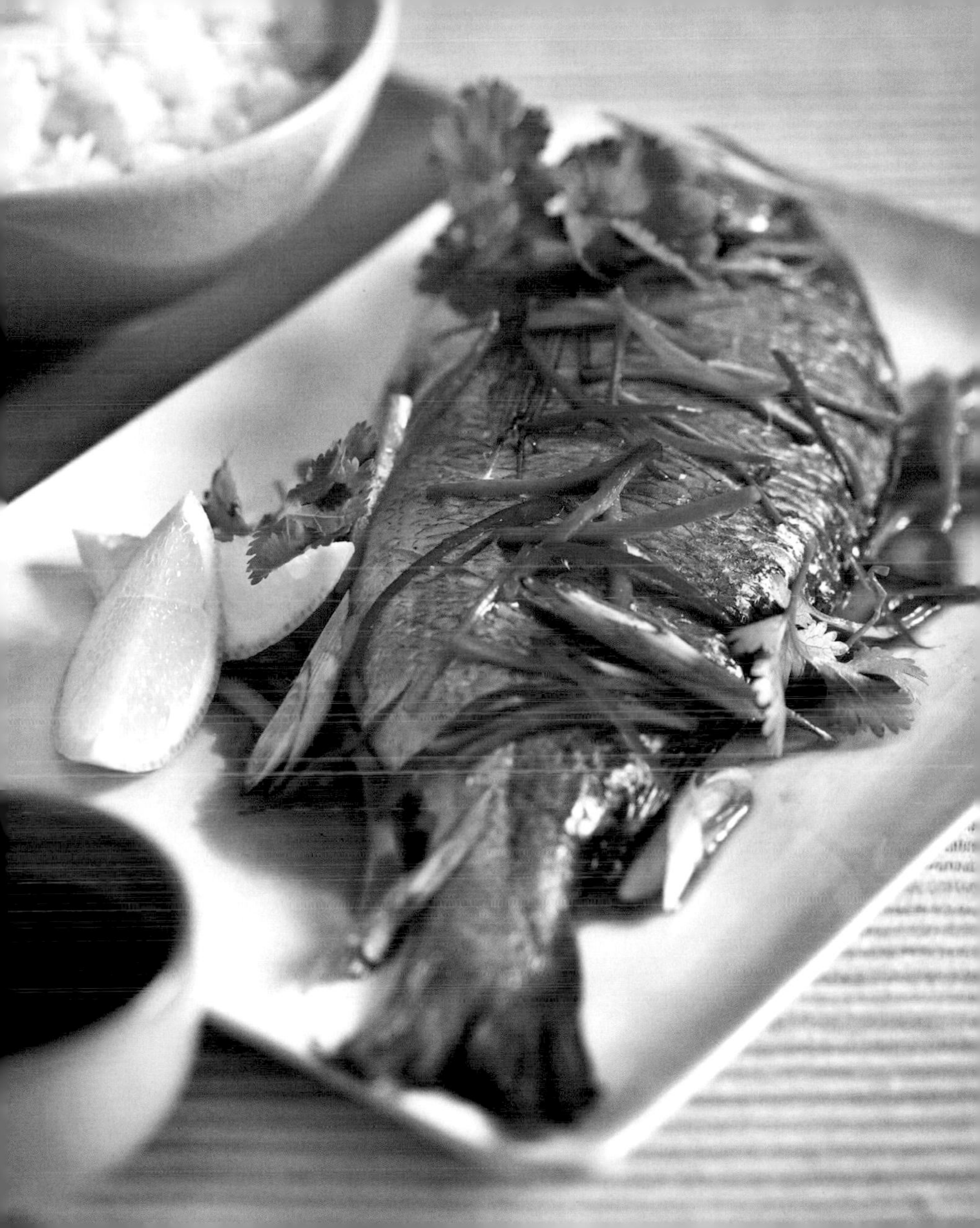

tuna steaks with wasabi dressing

Calories per serving **279**
Serves **4**
Preparation time **5 minutes**
Cooking time **6–7 minutes**

4 **tuna steaks**, about 150 g
(5 oz) each
2 teaspoons **mixed
peppercorns**, crushed
250 g (8 oz) **sugar snap peas**
1 teaspoon **toasted sesame
oil**
2 teaspoons **sesame seeds**,
lightly toasted

Dressing
2 tablespoons **light soy sauce**
4 tablespoons **mirin**
1 teaspoon **sugar**
1 teaspoon **wasabi paste**

Season the tuna steaks with the crushed peppercorns.
Heat a griddle pan over a medium-high heat and griddle
the tuna steaks for 2 minutes on each side until browned
but still pink in the centre. Remove from the pan and
leave to rest.

Put the sugar snap peas in a steamer basket and lower
into a shallow saucepan of boiling water so that the
peas are not quite touching the water. Drizzle with the
sesame oil, cover and steam for 2–3 minutes or until
tender. Alternatively, cook the peas in a bamboo or
electric steamer.

Place all of the dressing ingredients in a screw-top jar
and seal with a tight-fitting lid. Shake vigorously until
well combined.

Divide the sugar snap peas between 4 serving dishes,
then cut the tuna steaks in half diagonally and arrange
over the peas. Drizzle with the prepared dressing and
sprinkle with the sesame seeds. Serve immediately,
with cellophane rice noodles, if liked.

For tuna carpaccio, roll 500 g (1 lb) tuna fillet in the
peppercorns and seal on all sides in a very hot frying
pan. Cool, wrap in clingfilm and place in the freezer for
1 hour until semi-frozen. Remove and cut into very thin
slices. Arrange the slices on large plates and drizzle with
the dressing. Serve with the steamed and chilled sugar
snap peas, scattered with sesame seeds. **Calories per
serving 245**

thai-style beef salad

Calories per serving **253**
Serves **4**
Preparation time **20 minutes**
Cooking time **10 minutes**

125 g (4 oz) **green papaya**,
  peeled and deseeded
125 g (4 oz) **green mango**,
  peeled and stoned
handful of **mint leaves**,
  chopped
handful of **Thai basil leaves**
2 small, elongated **shallots**,
  finely sliced
1 tablespoon **vegetable oil**
4 **sirloin steaks**, about 125 g
  (4 oz) each

Dressing
1 cm (½ inch) piece of **fresh
  root ginger**, peeled and
  finely sliced
1½ tablespoons **palm sugar**
  or **soft light brown sugar**
½ **red chilli**, deseeded and
  finely sliced
juice of 2 **limes**
2 tablespoons **Thai fish sauce**

Grate or slice the papaya and mango into long, thin strips. Put the papaya and mango, mint and basil leaves in a large salad bowl and mix together, then stir in the shallots.

Make the dressing. Crush the ginger and sugar using a pestle and mortar. Add the chilli, lime juice and fish sauce, to taste.

Heat a griddle pan over a high heat, add the oil and fry the steaks for 5 minutes on each side or until cooked to the pinkness desired. Remove from the pan and leave to rest for 5 minutes.

Slice the steaks diagonally into thin slices and arrange on serving plates. Add the dressing to the salad, mix well to combine and serve with the steak.

For toasted rice khao koor, a special garnish you can add to this salad, put 3 tablespoons raw jasmine rice in a small frying pan over a medium heat, stirring continuously, until all the rice is golden in colour. Allow the rice to cool, then grind it coarsely in a spice grinder or using a pestle and mortar, and sprinkle over the finished salad. **Calories per serving 42**

steamed citrus sea bass

Calories per serving **256**
Serves **4**
Preparation time **15 minutes**
Cooking time **20 minutes**

1 whole **sea bream** or **sea
bass**, about 800–900 g
(1 lb 10 oz–2 lb), scaled
and gutted
50 ml (2 fl oz) **chicken stock**
or **water**
50 ml (2 fl oz) **Chinese rice
wine** or **dry sherry**
rind of 1 small **orange**, thinly
sliced
2.5 cm (1 inch) piece **fresh
root ginger**, thinly sliced
1 teaspoon **caster sugar**
3 tablespoons **light soy sauce**
½ teaspoon **sesame oil**
1 **garlic clove**, thinly sliced
3 **spring onions**, thinly sliced
1 tablespoon **groundnut oil**

Score 3 diagonal slits along each side of the fish with
a sharp knife, then cut in the opposite direction to make
a diamond pattern.

Cut 2 large pieces of foil about 1½ times the length of
the fish. Place the fish in the centre of the double layer
of foil and lift it up around the fish slightly. Pour the
stock and rice wine over the fish, then scatter with
the orange rind and half the ginger.

Place a circular rack inside a wok and pour in enough
water to come just below the top of the rack. Place the
lid on the wok and bring the water to a rolling boil.
Carefully sit the open fish parcel on the rack, cover
with the lid and steam for 15–18 minutes until the flesh
inside the slits is opaque. Carefully remove the fish from
the wok and place on a serving dish.

Stir the sugar into a bowl with the soy sauce and
sesame oil, then pour the liquid over the fish with the
garlic, spring onions and remaining ginger.

Heat the groundnut oil in a small frying pan over a
high heat until smoking hot, then pour it over the fish.
This will crisp up the spring onions and ginger and
release their aroma. Serve immediately.

**For steamed sea bream with mushrooms &
tomatoes**, place the fish on the foil as above and
season with salt and pepper. Top with 2 tablespoons
olive oil, 100 ml (3½ fl oz) dry white wine, 75 g (3 oz)
trimmed and sliced shiitake mushrooms and 6 halved
cherry tomatoes. Steam in the wok as above.
Calories per serving 292

spring minestrone

Calories per serving **221**
Serves **4**
Preparation time **15 minutes**
Cooking time **55 minutes**

2 tablespoons **olive oil**
1 **onion**, thinly sliced
2 **carrots**, peeled and diced
2 **celery sticks**, diced
2 **garlic cloves**, peeled
1 **potato**, peeled and diced
125 g (4 oz) **peas** or **broad
beans**, thawed if frozen
1 **courgette**, diced
125 g (4 oz) **green beans**,
trimmed and cut into 3.5 cm
(1½ inch) pieces
125 g (4 oz) **plum tomatoes**,
skinned and chopped
1.2 litres (2 pints) **vegetable
stock**
75 g (3 oz) **small pasta
shapes**
10 **basil leaves**, torn
salt and **pepper**

To serve
olive oil
grated **Parmesan cheese**

Heat the oil in a large, heavy-based saucepan over a low heat, add the onion, carrots, celery and garlic and cook, stirring occasionally, for 10 minutes. Add the potato, peas or broad beans, courgette and green beans and cook, stirring frequently, for 2 minutes. Add the tomatoes, season with salt and pepper and cook for a further 2 minutes.

Pour in the stock and bring to the boil, then reduce the heat and simmer gently for 20 minutes or until all the vegetables are very tender.

Add the pasta and basil to the soup and cook, stirring frequently, until the pasta is al dente. Season with salt and pepper to taste.

Ladle into bowls, drizzle with olive oil and sprinkle with the Parmesan. Serve with toasted country bread, if liked, or Parmesan toasts (see below).

For Parmesan toasts, to serve as an accompaniment, toast 4–6 slices of ciabatta on one side only under a preheated medium grill. Brush the other side with 2–3 tablespoons olive oil and sprinkle with chilli flakes and 2 tablespoons grated Parmesan cheese, then cook under the preheated grill until golden and crisp.
Calories per serving 185

plaice with herby coconut crust

Calories per serving **201**
Serves **4**
Preparation time **5 minutes**
Cooking time **15 minutes**

30 g (1 ½ oz) **desiccated
 coconut**
50 g (2 oz) **breadcrumbs**
2 tablespoons chopped
 chives
pinch of **paprika**
4 **skinless plaice fillets**
salt and **pepper**
lime wedges, to serve

Mix together the coconut, breadcrumbs, chives and paprika and season to taste.

Arrange the fish fillets on a baking sheet, top each one with some of the coconut mixture and cook in a preheated oven, 180°C (350°F), Gas Mark 4, for 15 minutes.

Serve the fish with lime wedges and accompanied with baked potatoes and a rocket salad, if liked.

For lemon sole with an almond crust, substitute the plaice fillets for 4 skinless lemon sole fillets. In the topping, use 50 g (2 oz) flaked almonds instead of coconut. Serve the fish with new potatoes, watercress and lemon wedges. **Calories per serving 232**

poached sea bass & salsa

Calories per serving **205**
Serves **4**
Preparation time **15 minutes**
Cooking time **25 minutes**

5 cm (2 inch) piece of **fresh root ginger**, peeled and thinly sliced
2 **lemon grass stalks**, sliced lengthways
1 **lime**, sliced
200 ml (7 fl oz) **dry sherry**
2 tablespoons **fish sauce**
2 **sea bass**, about 625 g (1 ¼ lb) each, cleaned and scaled

Salsa
3 firm **tomatoes**
1 **lemon grass stalk**, outer leaves discarded, finely sliced
1.25 cm (½ inch) piece of **fresh root ginger**, peeled and finely grated
2 tablespoons chopped **coriander**
2 **spring onions**, chopped
2 teaspoons **groundnut oil**
1 tablespoon **lime juice**
1 ½ teaspoons **light soy sauce**

Put the ginger, lemon grass, lime, sherry, fish sauce and enough water to just cover the fish in a fish kettle or large frying pan. Bring to the boil, then reduce the heat and simmer gently for 5 minutes.

Place the sea bass in the fish kettle or on a large piece of nonstick baking paper if using a frying pan. Lower into the stock, adding more water if necessary so that it covers the fish. Bring the stock to the boil and then turn off the heat. Cover and leave to poach for 15 minutes or until the fish flakes easily when pressed in the centre with a knife.

Meanwhile, make the salsa. Deseed and finely dice the tomatoes and place in a bowl with the lemon grass, ginger, coriander and spring onions. Stir through the oil, lime juice and soy sauce and leave to infuse.

Lift the poached sea bass carefully from the cooking liquid on to a plate. Peel away the skin and gently lift the fillets from the bones. Place on a serving dish with the salsa and serve with steamed rice and lime wedges, if liked.

For pan-fried sea bass with salsa, ask the fishmonger to fillet the whole sea bass. Heat 1 tablespoon olive oil in a nonstick frying pan and pan-fry the sea bass fillets over a medium-high heat, skin side down, for 3–4 minutes. Reduce the heat, cover and cook for a further 3–4 minutes or until cooked through. Serve with the salsa. **Calories per serving 223**

thai red pork & bean curry

Calories per serving **216**
Serves **4**
Preparation time **10 minutes**
Cooking time **5 minutes**

2 tablespoons **groundnut oil**
1 ½ tablespoons ready-made
   Thai red curry paste
375 g (12 oz) **lean pork**,
   sliced into thin strips
100 g (7 oz) **French beans**,
   topped and cut in half
2 tablespoons **Thai fish sauce
   (nam pla)**
1 teaspoon **caster sugar**
Chinese chives or **regular
   chives**, to garnish

Heat the oil in a wok over a medium heat until the oil
starts to shimmer. Add the curry paste and cook, stirring,
until it releases its aroma.

Add the pork and French beans and stir-fry for 2–3
minutes until the meat is cooked through and the beans
are just tender.

Stir in the fish sauce and sugar and serve, garnished
with Chinese chives or regular chives.

For chicken green curry with sugar snap peas,
cook as above, replacing the red curry paste with
1 ½ tablespoons green curry paste, the pork with 375 g
(12 oz) sliced chicken breast and the French beans with
100 g (7 oz) sliced sugar snap peas. Add a dash of lime
juice before serving. **Calories per serving 204**

bass with tomato & basil sauce

Calories per serving **237**
Serves **4**
Preparation time **10 minutes**
Cooking time **30 minutes**

8 **plum tomatoes**, halved
2 tablespoons **lemon juice**
grated rind of 1 **lemon**, plus
 extra to garnish
4 **sea bass fillets**, about
 150 g (5 oz) each
2 tablespoons chopped **basil**
2 tablespoons **extra virgin
 olive oil**
salt and **pepper**

To garnish
basil leaves
lemon wedges

Make the sauce up to 2 days in advance. Arrange
the tomatoes in a roasting tin, season well and cook
in a preheated oven, 200°C (400°F), Gas Mark 6, for
20 minutes.

Transfer the tomatoes and any cooking juices to a pan
and heat through gently with the lemon juice and rind.
Season to taste and set aside until ready to serve.

Season the fish fillets and cook under a preheated hot
grill for approximately 10 minutes or until the fish
is cooked through.

Meanwhile, warm the sauce through. Stir the basil
and oil through the sauce and spoon it over the fish.
Garnish with basil leaves, more grated lemon rind
and lemon wedges.

For tiger prawns in tomato & basil sauce, replace
the bass fillets with 16 raw and peeled tiger prawns.
Fry the prawns in a little oil spray until pink and cooked
through. Make the sauce as above and spoon over
the top of the cooked prawns to serve. **Calories per
serving 169**

russian borshch

Calories per serving **259**
Serves **6**
Preparation time **15 minutes**
Cooking time **55 minutes**

25 g (1 oz) **butter**
1 tablespoon **sunflower oil**
1 **onion**, finely chopped
375 g (12 oz) uncooked
   beetroot, trimmed, peeled
   and diced
2 **carrots**, diced
2 **celery sticks**, diced
150 g (5 oz) **red cabbage**,
   cored and chopped
300 g (10 oz) **potatoes**, diced
2 **garlic cloves**, finely chopped
1.5 litres (2½ pints) **beef
   stock**
1 tablespoon **tomato purée**
6 tablespoons **red wine
   vinegar**
1 tablespoon **brown sugar**
2 **bay leaves**
salt and **pepper**

To serve
200 ml (7 fl oz) **soured cream**
small bunch of **dill**

Heat the butter and oil in a saucepan, add the onion and fry for 5 minutes until softened. Add the beetroot, carrot, celery, red cabbage, potatoes and garlic and fry for 5 minutes, stirring frequently.

Stir in the stock, tomato purée, vinegar and sugar. Add the bay leaves and season well with salt and pepper. Bring to the boil, then cover and simmer for 45 minutes until the vegetables are tender. Discard the bay leaves, then taste and adjust the seasoning if needed.

Ladle into bowls and top with spoonfuls of soured cream, torn dill fronds and a little black pepper. Serve with rye bread, if liked.

For vegetarian borshch with pinched dumplings, soak 40 g (1½ oz) dried mushrooms in 300 ml (½ pint) boiling water for 15 minutes. Make up the soup as above, omitting the beef stock, adding the soaked mushrooms and their liquid plus 1.2 litres (2 pints) vegetable stock instead. For the dumplings, mix 125 g (4 oz) white flour, ¼ teaspoon caraway seeds, salt and pepper, 2 beaten eggs and enough water to mix to a smooth dough. Shape into a sausage, pinch off pieces and add to the soup, simmering for 10 minutes until spongy. Omit the cream and dill and serve. **Calories per serving 277**

malaysian coconut vegetables

Calories per serving **251**
Serves **4**
Preparation time **15 minutes,**
   plus soaking
Cooking time **20 minutes**

125 g (4 oz) **broccoli florets**
125 g (4 oz) **French beans**,
   cut into 2.5 cm (1 inch)
   lengths
1 **red pepper**, cored,
   deseeded and sliced
125 g (4 oz) **courgettes**, thinly
   sliced

Coconut sauce
25 g (1 oz) tamarind pulp
150 ml (¼ pint) boiling **water**
400 ml (14 fl oz) can **coconut**
   milk
2 teaspoons **Thai green curry**
   paste
1.25 cm (½ inch) piece of
   fresh root ginger, peeled
   and finely grated
1 **onion**, cut into small cubes
½ teaspoon **ground turmeric**
salt

Make the coconut sauce. Put the tamarind in a bowl. Pour over the measurement water and leave to soak for 30 minutes. Mash the tamarind in the water, then push through a sieve set over another bowl, squashing the tamarind so that you get as much of the pulp as possible; discard the stringy bits and any seeds.

Take 2 tablespoons of the cream from the top of the coconut milk and pour it into a wok or large frying pan. Add the curry paste, ginger, onion and turmeric, and cook over a gentle heat, stirring, for 2–3 minutes. Stir in the rest of the coconut milk and the tamarind water. Bring to the boil, then reduce the heat to a simmer and add a pinch of salt.

Add the broccoli to the coconut sauce and cook for 5 minutes, then add the green beans and red pepper. Cook, stirring, for another 5 minutes. Finally, stir in the courgettes and cook gently for 1–2 minutes until the courgette is just tender. Serve immediately with some crispy prawn crackers, if liked.

For chicken & green beans in coconut sauce, soak the tamarind and make the coconut sauce as above. Add 500 g (1 lb) diced boneless, skinless chicken breast to the wok or frying pan. Simmer for 5 minutes, then add the sliced French beans, omitting the red pepper and courgettes. Simmer gently for another 5 minutes until the chicken is cooked through.
Calories per serving 365

cod & aubergine tapenade

Calories per serving **259**
Serves **4**
Preparation time **12 minutes**
Cooking time **35–40 minutes**

1 **aubergine**, cut into chunks
1 **garlic clove**, sliced
olive oil spray
4 thick, line-caught **cod fillets**,
   about 150 g (5 oz) each
finely grated rind of ½ **lemon**
2 teaspoons finely chopped
   lemon thyme
2 teaspoons **olive oil**
1–2 tablespoons **black olive
   tapenade**
1–2 tablespoons fat-free
   Greek yogurt
2 tablespoons **pine nuts**,
   lightly toasted (optional)
salt and **pepper**

Put the aubergine in a foil-lined roasting tin, scatter with the garlic, season with salt and pepper and spray with a little olive oil. Cover tightly with foil and place in a preheated oven, 180°C (350°F), Gas Mark 4, for 35–40 minutes or until the aubergine is tender.

Meanwhile, place a cod fillet in the centre of a piece of foil or nonstick baking paper. Scatter with a little lemon rind, lemon thyme and season with salt and pepper. Drizzle over ½ teaspoon of the olive oil, then fold the foil or paper over several times to make a small parcel. Repeat with the remaining cod fillets. Place the parcels on a baking sheet and bake in the oven 12 minutes before the end of the aubergine cooking time, until the fish is just cooked through. Leave to rest.

Remove the aubergine from the oven and place in a food processor or blender with the black olive tapenade and Greek yogurt. Blend until almost smooth, season to taste and scrape into a bowl.

Serve the cod on a bed of steamed green beans, scattered with the pine nuts, if using, and with the aubergine and yogurt purée on the side.

For baked lemon sole & capers, place 4 lemon sole fillets on a large, foil-lined baking sheet. Sprinkle with the lemon rind, lemon thyme and 1 teaspoon rinsed and drained capers, chopped. Drizzle with the olive oil, then season with pepper. Cover tightly with foil and place in the preheated oven for 8–10 minutes or until the fish is just cooked and flakes easily. Serve as above.
Calories per serving 262

recipes under 400 calories

moroccan grilled sardines

Calories per serving **302**
Serves **4**
Preparation time **10 minutes**
Cooking time **6–8 minutes**

12 **sardines**, cleaned and
  gutted
2 tablespoons **harissa**
2 tablespoons **olive oil**
juice of **1 lemon**
salt flakes and **pepper**
chopped coriander, to garnish
lemon wedges, to serve

Heat the grill on the hottest setting. Rinse the sardines and pat dry with kitchen paper. Make 3 deep slashes on both sides of each fish with a sharp knife.

Mix the harissa with the oil and lemon juice to make a thin paste. Rub into the sardines on both sides. Put the sardines on a lightly oiled baking sheet. Cook under the grill for 3–4 minutes on each side, depending on their size, or until cooked through. Season to taste with salt flakes and pepper and serve immediately garnished with coriander and with lemon wedges for squeezing over.

For baked sardines with pesto, line a medium ovenproof dish with 2 sliced tomatoes and 2 sliced onions. Prepare the sardines as above, then rub 4 tablespoons pesto over the fish and arrange in a single layer on top of the tomatoes and onions. Cover with foil and bake in a preheated oven, 200°C (400°F), Gas Mark 6, for 20–25 minutes or until the fish is cooked through. **Calories per serving 375**

beef fillet with red pepper crust

Calories per serving **302 (not including wholegrain rice)**
Serves **4**
Preparation time **15 minutes**
Cooking time **about 30 minutes**

1 **red pepper**, halved and deseeded
2 **garlic cloves**
8 dry **black olives**, pitted
1 tablespoon **olive oil**
2 teaspoons **capers**
8 **shallots**, peeled
50 ml (2 fl oz) **balsamic vinegar**
1 teaspoon **light muscovado sugar**
4 **beef fillet steaks**, about 150 g (5¼ oz) each
salt and **pepper**

Cook the pepper under a preheated hot grill until the skin blackens. Remove and cover with damp kitchen paper until it is cool enough to handle, then peel the skin off and chop.

Blend together the garlic, olives, 1 teaspoon oil, the capers and the chopped red pepper.

Put the shallots and the remaining oil in a small pan. Cover and cook, stirring frequently, over low heat for 15 minutes. Add the vinegar and sugar and cook uncovered, stirring frequently, for a further 5 minutes.

Season the steaks and cook, 2 at a time, in a preheated heavy-based frying pan or griddle pan. Cook on one side for 2 minutes, then transfer to a baking sheet. Top each steak with some red pepper mix. Bake in a preheated oven, 200°C (400°F), Gas Mark 6, for 5 minutes or according to taste. Leave to stand in a warm place for 5 minutes before serving with the balsamic shallots and, if liked, steamed wholegrain rice.

For beef fillet with mushroom crust, blend 350 g (11½ oz) chopped mushrooms with 2 crushed garlic cloves, 1 chopped onion, 1 tablespoon olive oil and seasoning. Cook as above for 10 minutes or until reduced down to concentrate. Add juice of ½ lemon, 2 tablespoons chopped fresh parsley and a dash of brandy, then cook for a further 5 minutes. Cook the steaks as above and top with the mushroom mixture. **Calories per serving 271**

chicken with red wine & grapes

Calories per serving **368**
Serves **4**
Preparation time **5 minutes**
Cooking time **30 minutes**

3 tablespoons **olive oil**
4 **skinless chicken breast fillets**, about 150 g (5 oz) each
1 **red onion**, sliced
2 tablespoons **red pesto** (see below for homemade)
300 ml (½ pint) **red wine**
300 ml (½ pint) **water**
125 g (4 oz) **red grapes**, halved and deseeded
salt and **black pepper**
basil leaves, to garnish

Heat 2 tablespoons of the oil in a large frying pan, add the chicken breasts and cook over a medium heat for 5 minutes, turning frequently, until browned all over. Remove from the pan with a slotted spoon and drain on kitchen paper.

Heat the remaining oil in the pan, add the onion slices and pesto and cook, stirring constantly, for 3 minutes until the onion is softened but not browned.

Add the wine and measurement water to the pan and bring to the boil. Return the chicken breasts to the pan and season with salt and pepper to taste. Reduce the heat and simmer for 15 minutes, or until the chicken is cooked through.

Stir in the grapes and serve immediately, garnished with basil leaves.

For homemade red pesto, put 1 chopped garlic clove, ½ teaspoon sea salt, 25 g (1 oz) basil leaves, 50 g (2 oz) drained sun-dried tomatoes in oil, 125 ml (4 fl oz) extra virgin olive oil and a little pepper in a food processor or blender and blend until smooth. Transfer to a bowl and stir in 2 tablespoons freshly grated Parmesan cheese. **Calories per serving 368**

hoisin pork stir-fry

Calories per serving **395**
Serves **2**
Preparation time **8 minutes**
Cooking time **6–8 minutes**

1 tablespoon **hoisin sauce**
1 tablespoon **light soy sauce**
1 tablespoon **white wine**
    vinegar
1 tablespoon **vegetable oil**
2 **garlic cloves**, sliced
1.25 cm (½ inch) piece of
    fresh root ginger, peeled
    and finely grated
1 small **red chilli**, deseeded
    and sliced
250 g (8 oz) **pork fillet**, thinly
    sliced
175 g (6 oz) **sugar snap peas**
175 g (6 oz) **broccoli florets**
2 tablespoons **water**

Combine the hoisin and soy sauces and vinegar in a bowl and set aside.

Heat the oil in a wok or large frying pan until starting to smoke, add the garlic, ginger and chilli and stir-fry over a high heat for 10 seconds. Add the pork fillet and stir-fry for 2–3 minutes until golden. Remove with a slotted spoon.

Add the sugar snap peas and broccoli florets to the pan and stir-fry for 1 minute. Add the measurement water and cook for a further 1 minute.

Return the pork to the pan, add the sauce mixture and cook for 1 minute until the vegetables are cooked. Serve with steamed rice.

For roasted hoisin pork, make the hoisin mixture as above. Brush the sauce over 4 pieces of pork fillet, about 175 g (6 oz) each, in a roasting tin and roast in a preheated oven, 200°C (400°F), Gas Mark 6, for 15 minutes. Leave to rest for 5 minutes, then serve with steamed green vegetables and boiled rice.
Calories per serving 428

spanish fish stew

Calories per serving **328**
Serves **4**
Preparation time **12 minutes**
Cooking time **about 25
  minutes**

2 tablespoons **olive oil**
1 large **red onion**, sliced
4 **garlic cloves**, chopped
1 teaspoon **smoked paprika**
  or **hot smoked paprika**
pinch of **saffron threads**
350 g (11½ oz) **monkfish
  fillet**, cut into chunks
250 g (8 oz) **red mullet fillets**,
  cut into large chunks
3 tablespoons **dry** or **medium-
  dry Madeira**
250 ml (8 fl oz) **fish** or
  vegetable stock
2 tablespoons **tomato purée**
400 g (13 oz) can **chopped
  tomatoes**
2 **bay leaves**
750 g (1½ lb) **live mussels**,
  scrubbed and debearded
  (discard any that don't shut
  when tapped) or 250 g (8 oz)
  cooked shelled mussels
salt and **pepper**
3 tablespoons chopped
  parsley, to garnish

Heat the oil in a large, heavy-based saucepan over
a medium-low heat, add the onion and garlic and cook
gently for 8–10 minutes or until softened.

Stir in the paprika and saffron and cook for a further
minute. Stir in the fish, then pour over the Madeira.
Add the stock, tomato purée, tomatoes and bay leaves
and season with salt and pepper. Bring to the boil, then
reduce the heat and simmer gently for 5 minutes.

Stir in the live mussels, cover and cook over a low
heat for about 3 minutes or until they have opened.
Discard any that remain closed. Alternatively, if using
cooked shelled mussels, simmer the stew for 2–3 minutes
more, or until the fish is cooked and tender, then stir in
the cooked mussels. Cook for 30 seconds or until the
mussels are heated through and piping hot.

Ladle into bowls and sprinkle with the parsley.
Serve immediately with crusty bread.

For pan-fried red mullet with tomato sauce,
cook the onion and garlic with the spices as above.
Pour in the Madeira and add the tomatoes, finely
grated rind of ½ lemon, a pinch of sugar and season
with salt and pepper. Simmer for 15–20 minutes. Heat
1–2 tablespoons olive oil in a nonstick frying pan, add
500 g (1 lb) red mullet fillets, skin side down, and fry
for 2–3 minutes or until crisp. Cover, reduce the heat
and cook for a further 2 minutes or until the fish is
just cooked through. Serve with the tomato sauce.
Calories per serving 330

crab & grapefruit salad

Calories per serving **384**
Serves **4**
Preparation time **10 minutes**

400 g (13 oz) **white crab meat**
1 **pink grapefruit**, peeled and sliced
50 g (2 oz) **rocket**
3 **spring onions**, sliced
200 g (7 oz) **mangetout**, halved
salt and **pepper**

Watercress dressing
85 g (3¼ oz) **watercress**, tough stalks removed
1 tablespoon **Dijon mustard**
2 tablespoon **olive oil**

To serve
4 **chapattis**
lime wedges

Combine the crab meat, grapefruit, rocket, spring onions and mangetout in a serving dish. Season to taste.

Make the dressing by blending together the watercress, mustard and oil. Season with salt.

Toast the chapattis. Stir the dressing into the salad and serve with the toasted chapattis and lime wedges on the side.

For prawn, potato & asparagus salad, substitute 400 g (13 oz) cooked peeled prawns for the crab and 100 g (3½ oz) cooked asparagus for the grapefruit, and add 200 g (7 oz) cooked and cooled potatoes. Calories per serving 343:

spiced beef & vegetable stew

Calories per serving **325**
Serves **4**
Preparation time **15 minutes**
Cooking time **2½ hours**

500 g (1 lb) **lean braising** or **stewing steak**
2 tablespoons **rapeseed** or **olive oil**
1 large **onion**, chopped
2.5 cm (1 inch) piece of **fresh root ginger**, peeled and finely grated
2 **chillies**, sliced
2 **garlic cloves**, crushed
600 ml (1 pint) **beef stock**
5 **star anise**
1 teaspoon **Chinese five-spice powder**
1 **cinnamon stick**
1 teaspoon **fennel seeds**
2 **dried kaffir lime leaves**
1 **lemon grass stalk**, chopped
1 teaspoon **black peppercorns**
2 tablespoons **shoyu** or **tamari sauce**
400 g (13 oz) **carrots**, cut into 1 cm (½ inch) slices
500 g (1 lb) **mooli** or **turnips**, cut into 1 cm (½ inch) slices
Chinese chives or **regular chives**, to garnish

Cut the steak into 2.5 cm (1 inch) cubes.

Heat the oil in a wok over a medium heat. Add the onion, ginger and chillies and stir-fry for 5–7 minutes.

Turn the heat up to high, add the beef and stir-fry for 5–10 minutes until lightly browned, stirring occasionally.

Add the garlic, stock, star anise, Chinese five-spice powder, cinnamon, fennel seeds, lime leaves, lemon grass, peppercorns and shoyu sauce and stir well. Bring the mixture back to the boil, then turn the heat down, cover the pan and simmer gently for 1½ hours, stirring occasionally. Add the carrots and mooli and continue cooking, covered, for another 45 minutes or until the vegetables have softened.

Skim any fat off the surface and garnish with the chives before serving.

For sesame broccoli, to accompany the stew, blanch 500 g (1 lb) broccoli florets in a saucepan of boiling water for 2 minutes, then drain and place on a serving dish. Make a dressing by combining 1 teaspoon sesame oil, 1 tablespoon shoyu sauce and 1 crushed garlic clove, and pour it over the broccoli. Just before serving, sprinkle the dish with 1 tablespoon toasted sesame seeds. **Calories per serving 69**

lamb fillet with vegetables

Calories per serving **317**
Serves **4**
Preparation time **20 minutes**
Cooking time **35–45 minutes**

500 g (1 lb) even-sized **baby new potatoes**
1 tablespoon chopped **rosemary**
400 g (13 oz) **lamb fillet**, diced
3 **garlic cloves**, halved
390 g (12½ oz) can **artichokes**, drained, rinsed and halved
1 **red pepper**, deseeded and quartered
200 g (7 oz) small **leeks**
salt and **pepper**

Put the potatoes in a pan with plenty of lightly salted water and bring to the boil. Drain immediately and toss with the rosemary.

Transfer the potatoes to a roasting tin with the lamb, garlic, artichokes and peppers. Cover and cook in a preheated oven, 180°C (350°F), Gas Mark 4, for 30–40 minutes or until cooked through and the potato skins are golden. Meanwhile, steam the leeks.

Drain the excess fat and serve the lamb with the roasted vegetables, leeks and any pan juices.

For herby baked lamb, before baking sprinkle the diced lamb with 6–8 tablespoons lemon juice, ¼ teaspoon each dried oregano and thyme, the leaves torn from 2 oregano sprigs, 4 lemon thyme sprigs and salt and pepper. **Calories per serving 319**

tuna layered lasagne

Calories per serving **335**
Serves **4**
Preparation time **10 minutes**
Cooking time **10 minutes**

8 dried **lasagne** sheets
1 tablespoon **olive oil**
1 bunch of **spring onions**, sliced
2 **courgettes**, diced
500 g (1 lb) **cherry tomatoes**, quartered
2 x 200 g (7 oz) cans **tuna** in water, drained
65 g (2½ oz) **wild rocket**
4 teaspoons **pesto**
pepper
basil leaves, to garnish

Cook the pasta sheets, in batches, in a large saucepan of salted boiling water according to the packet instructions until al dente. Drain and return to the pan to keep warm.

Meanwhile, heat the oil in a frying pan over a medium heat, add the spring onions and courgettes and cook, stirring, for 3 minutes. Remove the pan from the heat, add the tomatoes, tuna and rocket and gently toss everything together.

Place a little of the tuna mixture on 4 serving plates and top each with a pasta sheet. Spoon over the remaining tuna mixture, then top with the remaining pasta sheets. Season with plenty of pepper and top each with a spoonful of pesto and some basil leaves before serving.

For salmon lasagne, use 400 g (14 oz) salmon fillets. Pan-fry the fillets for 2–3 minutes on each side or until they are cooked through, remove the bones and skin, then flake and use in place of the tuna. **Calories per serving 443**

devilled fillet steaks

Calories per serving **336**
Serves **4**
Preparation time **10 minutes**
Cooking time **10 minutes**

2 tablespoons **olive oil**
4 **fillet steaks**, about 175 g
  (6 oz) each
2 tablespoons **balsamic
  vinegar**
75 ml (3 fl oz) **full-bodied red
  wine**
4 tablespoons **beef stock**
2 **garlic cloves**, chopped
1 teaspoon crushed **fennel
  seeds**
1 tablespoon **sun-dried
  tomato purée**
½ teaspoon **crushed dried
  chillies**
salt and **pepper**

To garnish
chopped **flat leaf parsley**
wild rocket leaves (optional)

Heat the oil in a nonstick frying pan until smoking hot. Add the steaks and cook over a very high heat for about 2–3 minutes on each side, if you want your steaks to be medium rare, 4–5 minutes for medium and 6–7 minutes for well done. Remove to a plate, season with salt and pepper and keep warm in a low oven.

Pour the vinegar, wine and stock into the pan and boil for 30 seconds, scraping any sediment from the base of the pan. Add the garlic and fennel seeds and whisk in the sun-dried tomato purée and crushed chillies. Bring the sauce to the boil and boil fast to reduce until syrupy.

Transfer the steaks to warmed serving plates, pouring any collected meat juices into the sauce. Return the sauce to the boil, then season with salt and pepper.

Pour the sauce over the steaks and serve immediately, garnished with chopped parsley and wild rocket leaves, if liked. Slice the steaks before serving, if you wish.

For devilled chicken breasts, heat the oil and use to cook 4 skinned chicken breasts for 5 minutes on each side. Leaving the chicken in the pan, follow the recipe above, replacing the beef stock with 4 tablespoons chicken stock and using ½ teaspoon dried oregano instead of the fennel seeds. **Calories per serving 276**

prawns & scallops with asparagus

Calories per serving **336**

Serves **4**

Preparation time **5 minutes**

Cooking time **10 minutes**

12 raw peeled **king prawns**

8 **scallops**

3 tablespoons **groundnut oil**

2.5 cm (1 inch) piece **fresh root ginger**, finely chopped

2 **garlic cloves**, crushed

250 g (8 oz) **asparagus**, cut into 2.5 cm (1 inch) lengths

2 tablespoons **Chinese rice wine** or **dry sherry**

1 tablespoon **malt vinegar**

1½ tablespoons **light soy sauce**

2 teaspoons **caster sugar**

100 ml (3½ fl oz) **water**

½ teaspoon **sesame oil**

salt and **white pepper**

Season the prawns and scallops with salt and freshly ground white pepper.

Heat 1 tablespoon of the oil in a wok over a high heat until the oil starts to shimmer. Add the prawns and stir-fry for 2 minutes until they begin to colour, then remove using a slotted spoon and set aside. Add another tablespoon of the oil to the wok and, once it is hot, stir-fry the scallops for 1 minute on each side. Remove using a slotted spoon and set aside.

Heat the remaining oil in the wok. Stir in the ginger, garlic and asparagus and stir-fry for 1 minute, then add the rice wine, vinegar, soy sauce, sugar and water and bring to the boil. Return the prawns and scallops to the wok and stir-fry until they are cooked and the asparagus is just tender. Add the sesame oil and give everything a good stir, then serve.

For king prawns with peppers & sesame seeds, use 16 raw peeled king prawns instead of the scallops. Replace the asparagus with 1 red and 1 yellow pepper, cored, deseeded and cut into thin strips. Cook as above, finishing with 2 tablespoons toasted sesame seeds. **Calories per serving 389**

gingery pork chops

Calories per serving **389**
Serves **4**
Preparation time **15 minutes**
Cooking time **20 minutes**

4 lean **pork chops**, about
    150 g (5 oz) each
3.5 cm (1½ inch) piece of
    fresh root ginger, peeled
    and grated
1 teaspoon **sesame oil**
1 tablespoon **dark soy sauce**
2 teaspoons **stem ginger
    syrup** or **runny honey**

Dressing
1½ tablespoons **light soy
    sauce**
juice of 1 **blood orange**
2 pieces of **stem ginger**, finely
    chopped

Salad
2 large **carrots**, peeled and
    coarsely grated
150 g (5 oz) **mangetout**,
    shredded
100 g (3½ oz) **bean sprouts**
2 **spring onions**, thinly sliced
2 tablespoons **unsalted
    peanuts**, roughly chopped
    (optional)

Place the pork in a shallow ovenproof dish and rub with the ginger, sesame oil, soy sauce and stem ginger syrup or honey until well covered. Leave them to to marinate for 10 minutes.

Make the dressing. Mix together all the ingredients in a bowl and set aside for the flavours to develop.

Cook the pork in a preheated oven, 180°C (350°F), Gas Mark 4, for 18–20 minutes or until cooked through but still juicy.

Meanwhile, mix the carrots, mangetout, bean sprouts and spring onions in a large bowl. Just before serving, toss with the dressing and pile into serving dishes. Sprinkle with the peanuts, if using, and top with the pork chops, drizzled with cooking juices. Serve immediately with steamed rice.

For pork & ginger stir-fry, replace the pork chops with 4 lean boneless pork loin steaks and thinly slice. Cut the carrots into matchsticks. Heat 1–2 teaspoons sesame oil in a hot wok or large frying pan, add the pork and stir-fry until just cooked. Add the carrots, mangetout, bean sprouts and spring onions and stir-fry for a further 1–2 minutes. Toss with the dressing and serve immediately, sprinkled with the peanuts, if liked.
Calories per serving 369

turkey & avocado salad

Calories per serving **345 (not including rye or flat bread)**
Serves **4**
Preparation time **15 minutes**

375 g (12 oz) cooked **turkey**
1 large **avocado**
punnet of **mustard and cress**
150 g (5 oz) **mixed salad leaves**
50 g (2 oz) **mixed toasted seeds**, such as **pumpkin** and **sunflower**

Dressing
2 tablespoons **apple juice**
2 tablespoons **natural yogurt**
1 teaspoon **clear honey**
1 teaspoon **wholegrain mustard**
salt and **pepper**

Thinly slice the turkey. Peel, stone and dice the avocado and mix it with the mustard and cress and salad leaves in a large bowl. Add the turkey and toasted seeds and stir to combine.

Make the dressing by whisking together the apple juice, yogurt, honey and mustard. Season to taste with salt and pepper.

Pour the dressing over the salad and toss to coat. Serve the salad with toasted wholegrain rye bread or rolled up in flat breads.

For crab, apple & avocado salad, prepare the salad in the same way, using 300 g (10 oz) cooked, fresh white crab meat instead of the turkey. Cut 1 apple into thin matchsticks and toss with a little lemon juice to stop it from discolouring. Make a dressing by whisking 2 tablespoons apple juice with 3 tablespoons olive oil, a squeeze of lemon juice and 1 finely diced shallot. Season to taste with salt and pepper. Pour the dressing over the salad, stir carefully to mix and serve. **Calories per serving 366**

plaice with sambal

Calories per serving **349**
Serves **4**
Preparation time **30 minutes,
    plus marinating**
Cooking time **30 minutes**

1 small **lemon grass stalk**
2 **garlic cloves**, crushed
6 tablespoons **grated fresh
    coconut**
2 **green chillies**, deseeded
    and finely chopped
4 **small whole plaice**, scaled
    and gutted
4 tablespoons **oil**

Sambal
1 **onion**, finely chopped
1 **garlic clove**, crushed
1 tablespoon **oil**
2 tablespoons **grated fresh
    coconut**
1 **red chilli**, deseeded and
    finely chopped
150 ml (¼ pint) **boiling water**
2 tablespoons **dried tamarind
    pulp**
2 teaspoons **caster sugar**
1 tablespoon **white wine
    vinegar**
1 tablespoon **chopped fresh
    coriander**

Finely chop the lemon grass stalk and mix with the garlic, coconut and green chillies. Smear this dry mixture over each plaice, then cover and leave to marinate in the refrigerator for 2 hours or overnight.

Make the coconut and tamarind sambal by gently frying the onion and garlic in the oil in a large frying pan until softened. Add the coconut with the red chilli, stir to coat in the oil and cook for 2–3 minutes. Pour the measurement water over the tamarind pulp in a heatproof bowl and stand for 10 minutes to dissolve.

Strain the juice from the tamarind pulp, mashing as much of the pulp through the sieve as possible. Add this juice to the pan with the sugar and simmer gently for 5 minutes. Add the vinegar, remove from the heat and leave to cool. When cold, stir in the chopped coriander. Turn into a bowl and wipe the pan clean.

Heat the oil in the pan and gently fry the plaice 2 at a time in the hot oil, turning once. After 6–8 minutes, when they are golden brown and cooked, remove from the oil and drain on kitchen paper. Keep warm while cooking the remaining fish. Serve the fish piping hot with the coconut and tamarind sambal.

For sugar snap salad to serve as an accompaniment, blanch 300 g (10 oz) sugar snap peas in boiling water for 1 minute, drain, refresh with cold water and thinly slice. Place in a bowl with 3 chopped spring onions, 1 tablespoon chopped coriander leaves and 1 tablespoon chopped mint. Drizzle with a dressing made from ½ a small finely sliced red chilli, 2 tablespoons lime juice, 1 tablespoon fish sauce and 1 tablespoon caster sugar. **Calories per serving 45**

beef strips with radicchio

Calories per serving **353**
Serves **4**
Preparation time **5 minutes**
Cooking time **5 minutes**

3 **sirloin steaks**, about 300 g
   (10 oz) each
½ tablespoon **olive oil**
2 **garlic cloves**, finely chopped
150 g (5 oz) **radicchio**, sliced
   into 2.5 cm (1 inch) strips
salt

Trim the fat from the steaks and slice the meat into very thin strips.

Heat the oil in a heavy-based frying pan over a high heat, add the garlic and steak strips, season with salt and stir-fry for 2 minutes or until the steak strips are golden brown.

Add the radicchio and stir-fry until the leaves are just beginning to wilt. Serve immediately.

For beef & caramelized onion couscous salad, brush 700 g (1¼ lb) beef fillet with 1 tablespoon olive oil, then sprinkle well with pepper. Heat a nonstick frying pan over a medium-high heat and cook the beef for 4 minutes on each side or until seared all over but still rare inside. Remove from the pan and leave to rest. To make the onion couscous, heat 2 tablespoons olive oil in the pan over a medium heat, add 4 sliced onions and fry, stirring occasionally, for 8–10 minutes or until softened. Meanwhile, put 200 g (7 oz) couscous in a heatproof bowl and pour over 350 ml (12 fl oz) boiling chicken or beef stock. Cover and leave to stand for 5 minutes or according to the packet instructions, until the stock has been absorbed, then fluff up with a fork. Mix together 2 tablespoons Dijon mustard, 1 tablespoon olive oil, the juice of 1 lemon and salt and pepper and toss with the couscous and onions. Slice the beef and place on top of the couscous. Serve with some rocket leaves on the side. **Calories per serving 498**

prawns with garlicky beans

Calories per serving **389**
Serves **4**
Preparation time **10 minutes**
Cooking time **15 minutes**

3 tablespoons **olive oil**
1 **large onion**, finely chopped
3 **garlic cloves**, crushed
2 x 400 g (13 oz) cans
  cannellini, haricot or **butter beans**, drained
100 ml (3½ fl oz) **vegetable** or **fish stock**
400 g (13 oz) raw **peeled prawns**
½ teaspoon **mild sweet paprika**
2 tablespoons **sun-dried tomato paste**
1 tablespoon chopped **oregano**
2 teaspoons **clear honey**
pepper

Heat 2 tablespoons of the oil in a saucepan, add the onion and fry gently for 5 minutes. Add the garlic and fry for a further minute.

Remove the pan from the heat. Tip in the beans and use a potato masher to crush them. Add the stock and plenty of pepper and set aside.

Dust the prawns with the paprika and a little salt. Heat the remaining oil in a frying pan, add the prawns and fry for 5–6 minutes, turning once or twice during cooking, until they turn pink and are cooked through. Stir in the tomato paste, oregano, honey and 2 tablespoons water and cook for 2–3 minutes or until it begins to bubble.

Meanwhile, reheat the pan with the beans until piping hot. Spoon the bean mixture into small dishes, pile the prawns on top and pour over the cooking juices.

For blackened cod with garlicky beans, prepare and cook the beans as above. Spread one side of each of 4 x 175g (6oz) cod fillets with 1 heaped teaspoon of ready-made black olive tapenade. Heat 2 tablespoons olive oil in a griddle pan over a medium heat, add the fish and cook for about 5 minutes on each side or until cooked through. Serve on a bed of crushed beans, and sprinkle with chopped black olives and parsley. **Calories per serving 331**

chicken & tofu miso noodles

Calories per serving **359**
Serves **4**
Preparation time **10 minutes**
Cooking time **25 minutes**

2 x 10 g sachets **instant miso soup powder** or **paste**
750 ml (1¼ pints) **water**
2 **star anise**
2 tablespoons **fish sauce**
1 tablespoon **light soy sauce**
1 tablespoon **palm sugar** or **soft light brown sugar**
1 **red chilli**, deseeded and sliced (optional)
200 g (7 oz) **baby corn**
125 g (4 oz) **mangetout**
250 g (8 oz) **cooked chicken breast**, torn
200 g (7 oz) **firm silken tofu**, cut into 1 cm (½ inch) cubes
160 g (5½ oz) **enoki mushrooms**, or **shiitake mushrooms**, thinly sliced
400 g (13 oz) **fresh egg noodles**
1 **spring onion**, very finely sliced, to garnish (optional)

Place the miso powder or paste in a large saucepan with the measurement water, star anise, fish sauce, soy sauce, sugar and chilli, if using. Bring to the boil, then reduce the heat and simmer gently for 15 minutes.

Stir in the baby corn and mangetout and cook for a further 3 minutes or until almost tender. Remove the pan from the heat, stir in the chicken, tofu and mushrooms and cover to retain the heat.

Cook the noodles in a large saucepan of boiling water for 3–4 minutes, or according to the packet instructions, until tender. Drain well and divide between deep bowls, then ladle over the hot soup and serve immediately, garnished with the spring onion, if liked.

For chicken, tofu & mushroom stir-fry, heat 2 tablespoons groundnut oil in a smoking hot wok or large frying pan. Stir-fry the baby corn and mangetout for 2 minutes or until beginning to wilt. Add the chicken, tofu and mushrooms and stir-fry for 1–2 minutes or until hot and the mushrooms are tender. Stir in a 350 g (11½ oz) jar of black bean stir-fry sauce, toss briefly and serve with the cooked noodles, sprinkled with spring onions. **Calories per serving 470**

korean beef with cucumber

Calories per serving **362**
Serves **4**
Preparation time **12 minutes,
plus marinating**
Cooking time **10 minutes**

500 g (1 lb) **sirloin steak**,
trimmed and cut into thin
strips
2 teaspoons **sesame oil**
2 tablespoons **light soy sauce**
½ teaspoon **salt**
1 teaspoon **caster sugar**
2 **garlic cloves**, crushed
1 tablespoon chopped **fresh
root ginger**
1 **cucumber**
3 tablespoons **groundnut oil**
4 **spring onions**, finely sliced
on the diagonal
2 tablespoons toasted
sesame seeds, to garnish

Marinate the beef for 30 minutes in a bowl with the sesame oil, soy sauce, salt, sugar, garlic and ginger.

Peel the cucumber, cut it in half lengthways and then into 1cm (½ inch) slices.

Heat half the oil in a wok over a high heat until the oil starts to shimmer. Add half the beef and stir-fry for 2–3 minutes, until just cooked, then remove using a slotted spoon.

Heat the remaining oil and stir-fry the rest of the beef in the same way.

Add the cucumber and spring onions. Stir-fry for a further 1 minute, until the cucumber is only slightly tender, and serve garnished with a scattering of toasted sesame seeds.

For spiced pork with cucumber, replace the beef with 500 g (1 lb) lean pork, cut into strips. Add 1 tablespoon crushed coriander seeds to the marinade ingredients and prepare the dish as above. Finish by tossing 1 red chilli, cut into thin rounds, a handful of coriander leaves and the juice of ½ lime into the finished dish.
Calories per serving 346

chinese style turkey wraps

Calories per serving **365**
Serves **2**
Preparation time **10 minutes**
Cooking time **1–2 minutes**

½ teaspoon **vegetable oil**
100 g (3½ oz) **turkey breast**,
   thinly sliced
1 tablespoon **clear honey**
2 tablespoons **soy sauce**
1 tablespoon **sesame oil**
2 soft **flour tortillas**
50 g (2 oz) **bean sprouts**
¼ **red pepper**, cored,
   deseeded and thinly sliced
¼ **onion**, thinly sliced
25 g (1 oz) **mangetout**, sliced
2 **baby sweetcorn**, thinly
   sliced

Heat the oil in a frying pan over a moderate heat and add the turkey to the pan. Stir for 1–2 minutes until cooked through. Reduce the heat and stir in the honey, soy sauce and sesame oil, making sure that the turkey is well coated. Set aside to cool.

Assemble a wrap by placing half the turkey mixture down the centre of a tortilla. Add half the bean sprouts and pepper, onion, mangetout and baby sweetcorn. Repeat with the other tortilla. (Alternatively, retain the remaining tortilla and mixture for use another day; the mixture will keep for up to 24 hours in the refrigerator.)

Roll up the tortilla securely and wrap in nonstick baking paper (clingfilm can make the wrap rather soggy).

For Chinese-style pork & pak choi wraps, replace the turkey with 125 g (4 oz) tenderloin pork strips tossed with ½ teaspoon Chinese five spice and cook as above for 3–4 minutes. Add 1 small head pak choi, shredded with the honey, soy sauce and sesame oil and cook for a further 2 minutes. Assemble as above with 125 g (4 oz) beansprouts, omitting the mangetout, onion and sweetcorn. **Calories per serving 389**

grilled lamb with caperberries

Calories per serving **308**
Serves **4**
Preparation time **10 minutes**
Cooking time **10 minutes**

4 **lamb leg steaks**, about
125 g (4 oz) each, fat
trimmed off
6 tablespoons chopped **flat
leaf parsley**, plus extra
whole sprigs to garnish
1 **garlic clove**, crushed
12 **sun-dried tomatoes**
1 tablespoon **lemon juice**
1 tablespoon **olive oil**
2 tablespoons **caperberries**,
rinsed
salt and **pepper**

Season the meat and cook under a preheated hot grill for about 5 minutes on each side until golden.

Reserve 4 tablespoons of the chopped parsley. Blend the remaining parsley with the garlic, tomatoes, lemon juice and oil.

Spoon the tomato sauce over the lamb. Sprinkle over the reserved chopped flat leaf parsley and add the caperberries. Garnish with whole parsley sprigs and serve with pasta, if liked.

For grilled lamb with tapenade, use black olive tapenade instead of the dressing and stir all the parsley through it. To make your own tapenade, whiz 150 g (5 oz) pitted black olives, 3 tablespoons extra virgin olive oil, 1 garlic clove and 2 salted anchovies in a food processor with black pepper and add chopped flat leaf parsley to taste. **Calories per serving 357**

chicken & aduki bean salad

Calories per serving **376**
Serves **4**
Preparation time **15 minutes**
Cooking time **2–3 minutes**

1 **green pepper**, cored,
  deseeded and chopped
1 **red pepper**, cored,
  deseeded and chopped
1 small **red onion**, finely
  chopped
400 g (13 oz) can **aduki
  beans**, drained
200 g (7 oz) can **sweetcorn**,
  drained
1 small bunch of **coriander**,
  chopped
50 g (2 oz) unsweetened
  coconut chips or **flakes**
250 g (8 oz) cooked **chicken
  breast**, shredded
small handful of **alfalfa shoots**
  (optional)

Dressing
3 tablespoons **light
  groundnut oil**
2 tablespoons **light soy sauce**
2.5 cm (1 inch) piece of **fresh
  root ginger**, peeled and
  finely grated
1 tablespoon **rice vinegar**

Mix together the green and red peppers, onion, aduki beans, sweetcorn and half the coriander in a large bowl. Whisk together the dressing ingredients in a separate bowl, then stir 3 tablespoons into the bean salad. Spoon the salad into serving dishes.

Place the coconut chips or flakes in a nonstick frying pan over a medium heat and dry-fry for 2–3 minutes or until lightly golden brown, stirring continuously.

Scatter the shredded chicken and remaining coriander leaves over the bean salad and sprinkle with the toasted coconut and alfalfa shoots, if using. Serve with the remaining dressing.

For prawn, avocado & coconut salad, make as above, replacing the chicken with 250 g (8 oz) cooked, peeled prawns. Dice the flesh of 1 firm, ripe avocado, toss in 1 tablespoon of lime juice and add to the bean salad. Serve as above. **Calories per serving 458**

quick tuna steak with green salsa

Calories per serving **383 (not including crusty bread)**

Serves **4**

Preparation time **14 minutes, plus marinating**

Cooking time **2–4 minutes**

2 tablespoons **olive oil**

grated rind of 1 **lemon**

2 teaspoons chopped **parsley**

½ teaspoon crushed **coriander seeds**

4 fresh **tuna steaks**, about 150 g (5 oz) each

salt and **pepper**

Salsa

2 tablespoons **capers**, chopped

2 tablespoons chopped **cornichons**

1 tablespoon finely chopped **parsley**

2 teaspoons chopped **chives**

2 teaspoons finely chopped **chervil**

30 g (1½ oz) pitted **green olives**, chopped

1 **shallot**, finely chopped (optional)

2 tablespoons **lemon juice**

2 tablespoons **olive oil**

Mix together the oil, lemon rind, parsley and coriander seeds with plenty of pepper in a bowl. Rub the tuna steaks with the mixture.

Combine the ingredients for the salsa, season to taste and set aside.

Heat a griddle or frying pan until hot and cook the tuna steaks for 1–2 minutes on each side to cook partially. The tuna should be well seared but rare. Remove and allow to rest for a couple of minutes.

Serve the tuna steaks with a spoonful of salsa, a dressed lettuce salad and plenty of fresh crusty bread.

For yellow pepper & mustard salsa, combine the following: 2 yellow peppers, finely chopped; 1 tablespoon Dijon mustard; 2 tablespoons each finely chopped chives, parsley and dill; 1 teaspoon sugar; 1 tablespoon cider vinegar and 2 tablespoons olive oil. **Calories per serving 46**

spicy pork, fried rice & greens

Calories per serving **384**

Serves **4**

Preparation time **15 minutes,
  plus marinating**

Cooking time **20 minutes**

200 g (7 oz) **easy-cook
  basmati rice**

3 tablespoons **hoisin sauce**

2 **garlic cloves**, crushed

5 cm (2 inch) piece **fresh root
  ginger**, grated

1 **red chilli**, sliced

1 **star anise**

1 tablespoon **sun-dried
  tomato purée**

300 g (10 oz) **pork fillet**, cut
  into thin strips

sunflower oil spray

1 **red onion**, chopped

125 g (4 oz) **cabbage** or
  spring greens, finely
  chopped

1 **carrot**, finely sliced

toasted sesame seeds,
  to serve

Mix together the hoisin sauce, garlic, ginger, chilli, star anise and tomato purée. Toss the pork in the mixture, cover and set aside for up to 1 hour.

Meanwhile, cook the rice in boiling salted water for 16–18 minutes. Drain and set aside.

Heat a wok over high heat and spray with oil. Remove the pork from the marinade (discard the remainder) and cook the meat in the wok for about 1 minute. Stir in the onion, cabbage and carrot, then the rice. Toss and stir everything together over high heat for about 3 minutes, until the rice is hot. Sprinkle with sesame seeds and serve.

For hoisin lamb with stir-fry noodles, use 300 g (10 oz) lamb fillet instead of pork and omit the rice and tomato purée. Marinate and stir-fry the lamb with the vegetables as above. Then add 3 x 150 g (5 oz) packets straight-to-wok rice noodles (or dried rice noodles, cooked according to the packet instructions) and stir-fry for about 1 minute, until hot. Sprinkle with chopped fresh coriander leaves instead of sesame seeds and serve. **Calories per serving 345**

king prawns with japanese salad

Calories per serving **388**
Serves **4**
Preparation time **10 minutes,
plus cooling**
Cooking time **3 minutes**

400 g (13 oz) raw, peeled
king prawns
200 g (7 oz) **bean sprouts**
125 g (4 oz) **mangetout**,
shredded
100 g (3½ oz) **water
chestnuts**, thinly sliced
½ **iceberg lettuce**, shredded
12 **radishes**, thinly sliced
1 tablespoon **sesame seeds**,
lightly toasted

Dressing
2 tablespoons **rice vinegar**
125 ml (4 fl oz) **sunflower oil**
1 teaspoon **five spice powder**
(optional)
2 tablespoons **mirin**

Set a steamer over a pan of simmering water and steam the king prawns for 2–3 minutes until cooked and pink. Set aside and leave to cool.

Make the dressing by mixing together all the ingredients in a small bowl.

Toss together the bean sprouts, mangetout, water chestnuts, lettuce and radishes and scatter over the prawns and sesame seeds. Drizzle over the dressing and serve immediately.

For chilli sauce to serve as an accompaniment, combine 1 finely chopped garlic clove, ½ teaspoon finely grated fresh root ginger, 2 teaspoons light soy sauce, 1 tablespoon sweet chilli sauce and ½ tablespoon tomato ketchup. Mix well. **Calories per serving 19**

haddock parcels & coconut rice

Calories per serving **340**
Serves **4**
Preparation time **15 minutes**
Cooking time **20 minutes**

4 **haddock fillets**, about
    150 g (5 oz) each
4 tablespoons chopped **fresh**
    coriander
1 **red chilli**, chopped
1 **shallot**, finely sliced
1 **lime**, sliced, plus extra lime
    halves to serve
2 **lemon grass stalks**,
    1 roughly chopped and
    1 bashed
200 g (7 oz) **Thai jasmine**
    rice
2 fresh or dried **kaffir lime**
    leaves
50 ml (2 fl oz) **reduced-fat**
    coconut milk

Cut 4 pieces of nonstick baking paper, each 30 cm
(12 inches) square. Put a haddock fillet in the centre
of each piece and arrange some of the coriander, chilli,
shallot, lime and chopped lemon grass stalk evenly over
each. Wrap them up into neat parcels.

Transfer the parcels to a baking sheet and cook in
a preheated oven, 180°C (350°F), Gas Mark 4, for
20 minutes.

Meanwhile, put the rice in a pan with 400 ml (14 fl oz)
water, the bashed lemon grass stalk and the lime
leaves. Cover and simmer for 12 minutes. When the
rice is cooked and the water absorbed, stir in the
coconut milk. Serve with the haddock parcels, with
some extra lime halves.

For salmon parcels with sesame rice, use 150 g
(5 oz) portions of skinless salmon fillet instead of the
haddock. Use lemon slices instead of lime and omit
the lemon grass. Sprinkle a few drops of sesame oil
over each salmon portion and cook as above. Omit
the lime leaves and coconut milk from the rice. Fork
2 tablespoons toasted sesame seeds and 2 chopped
spring onions into the cooked rice and serve with
the salmon, adding lemon wedges for more zest.
Calories per serving 493

tomato & chorizo stew with clams

Calories per serving **355**
Serves **4**
Preparation time **15 minutes**
Cooking time **about**
  25 minutes

225 g (8 oz) **chorizo** sausage,
  cut into chunks
1 teaspoon **coriander seeds**,
  crushed
1 tablespoon **fennel seeds**,
  crushed
1 **onion**, finely chopped
1 **red chilli**, deseeded and
  finely chopped
2 **garlic cloves**, finely chopped
50 ml (2 fl oz) **white wine**
400 g (13 oz) can **chopped**
  tomatoes
200 ml (7 fl oz) **fish stock**
500 g (1 lb) **live clams**,
  cleaned (discard any that
  don't shut when tapped)
small handful of **basil leaves**,
  to garnish

Heat a large saucepan over a high heat, add the chorizo
and fry until the natural oil has been released and the
chorizo is beginning to colour. Remove with a slotted
spoon, leaving behind the oil, and set aside.

Add the coriander and fennel seeds to the chorizo oil
and fry for 1 minute, then add the onion and chilli and
fry until the onion has softened but not coloured. Add
the garlic and fry for a further minute.

Pour in the white wine and leave to bubble until just
1 tablespoon of liquid is left. Add the tomatoes and
stock and bring to the boil, then return the chorizo to
the pan. Tip in the clams, then cover and cook until the
clams have opened. Discard any that remain closed.

Ladle into bowls, sprinkle with a few basil leaves and
serve with crusty bread, if liked.

For spicy bean stew with pan-fried John Dory,
make the stew as above, omitting the clams and chorizo
and adding a 400 g (13 oz) can haricot beans and a
400 g (13 oz) can kidney beans, drained. Pan-fry
2 John Dory fillets and serve with the bean stew.
Calories per serving 259

pork with red pepper & noodles

Calories per serving **314**
Serves **4**
Preparation time **30 minutes**
Cooking time **10 minutes**

150 g (5 oz) **flat rice noodles**
sunflower oil spray
3 **spring onions**, sliced
1 **red pepper**, diced
2 **kaffir lime leaves**, shredded
2 **red chillies**, deseeded and
    sliced
½ **lemon grass stalk**, finely
    chopped
450 g (14½ oz) **pork fillet**,
    shredded
2 tablespoons **soy sauce**
175 ml (6 fl oz) **Thai fish
    sauce** (nam pla)
65 g (2½ oz) **palm sugar** or
    soft brown sugar

To garnish
red or **green basil leaves**
shredded spring onions

Cook the noodles according to the instructions on the packet.

Heat a wok or large frying pan and lightly spray with oil. Add the spring onions, red pepper, lime leaves, chillies and lemon grass and stir-fry for 1 minute.

Add the shredded pork and stir-fry over high heat for 2 minutes. Add the soy sauce, fish sauce, sugar and drained noodles and cook for about 2 minutes, using 2 spoons to lift and stir until the noodles are evenly coated and hot.

Serve immediately, garnished with basil leaves and shredded spring onions.

For pork with red pepper, orange & honey, omit the lime leaves, lemon grass stalk, fish sauce and sugar. Stir-fry the pork as above with the spring onions, red pepper and chillies, then add the soy sauce, grated rind of 1 orange and 3 teaspoons each fresh orange juice and honey. Add the drained noodles and cook as above. Serve garnished with orange wedges. **Calories per serving 319**

swordfish with couscous & salsa

Calories per serving **399**
Serves **4**
Preparation time **10 minutes**
Cooking time **10 minutes**

4 **swordfish steaks**, about
  150 g (5 oz) each
4–5 small ripe **tomatoes**
16 **Kalamata olives** in brine,
  drained
2 tablespoons chopped **flat
  leaf parsley**
salt and **pepper**
200 g (7 oz) **couscous**

Season the swordfish steaks with salt and pepper.

Dice or quarter the tomatoes and transfer them to a
bowl with all the juices. Remove the stones from the
olives and chop the flesh if the pieces are still large.
Stir them into the tomatoes with parsley, season to
taste and set aside.

Cook the couscous according to the instructions on
the packet and set aside.

Meanwhile, cook the swordfish steaks, 2 at a time,
in a preheated hot griddle pan. Cook on the first side for
4 minutes, without disturbing them, then turn and cook
for a further minute.

Serve the swordfish and couscous immediately, topped
with the olive and tomato salsa.

For hake with pasta & salsa, replace the couscous
with 200 g (7 oz) tagliatelle or baby pasta shapes and
cook according to the packet instructions. Replace the
swordfish with 4 hake fillets and cook as described
above. When the pasta is cooked, toss with the chopped
parsley and a handful of chopped capers. Serve the
hake and pasta as above, topped with the salsa.
Calories per serving 366

recipes
under 500
calories

falafel pitta pockets

Calories per serving **470**
Serves **4**
Preparation time **15 minutes,
    plus overnight soaking**
Cooking time **12 minutes**

250 g (8 oz) **dried chickpeas**
1 **small onion**, finely chopped
2 **garlic cloves**, crushed
½ bunch of **parsley**
½ bunch of **coriander**
2 teaspoons **ground
    coriander**
½ teaspoon **baking powder**
2 tablespoons **vegetable oil**,
    for shallow-frying
4 **wholemeal pitta breads**
handful of **salad leaves**
2 **tomatoes**, diced
4 tablespoons **fat-free Greek
    yogurt**
salt and **pepper**

Put the chickpeas in a bowl, add cold water to cover by a generous 10 cm (4 inches) and leave to soak overnight.

Drain the chickpeas, transfer to a food processor and process until coarsely ground. Add the onion, garlic, fresh herbs, ground coriander and baking powder. Season with salt and pepper and process until really smooth. Using wet hands, shape the mixture into 16 small patties.

Heat the vegetable oil in a large frying pan over a medium-high heat, add the patties, in batches, and fry for 3 minutes on each side or until golden and cooked through. Remove with a slotted spoon and drain on kitchen paper.

Split the pitta breads and fill with the falafel, salad leaves and diced tomatoes. Add a spoonful of the yogurt to each and serve immediately.

For falafel salad, toss 4 handfuls of mixed salad leaves with a little olive oil, lemon juice and salt and pepper and arrange on serving plates. Core, deseed and dice 1 red pepper and sprinkle it over the salads. Top with the falafel and spoon over a little yogurt.
Calories per serving 305

prawn, mango & avocado wrap

Calories per serving **409**
Serves **4**
Preparation time **10 minutes,
plus standing**

2 tablespoons **low-fat crème
fraîche**
2 teaspoons **tomato ketchup**
few drops of **Tabasco sauce,**
to taste
300 g (10 oz) cooked peeled
prawns
1 **mango**, peeled, stoned and
thinly sliced
1 **avocado**, peeled, stoned
and sliced
4 flour **tortillas**
100 g (3½ oz) **watercress**

Mix together the crème fraîche, ketchup and Tabasco to taste in a bowl.

Add the prawns, mango and avocado and toss the mixture together.

Spoon the mixture into the tortillas, add some sprigs of watercress, roll up and serve.

For tangy chicken wraps, marinate 300 g (10 oz) chicken in a mixture of 1 tablespoon fresh lemon or lime juice, I tablespoon Worcestershire sauce and 1 chopped garlic clove for 20 minutes. Cook the chicken under a preheated medium grill for 10 minutes, turning often. Slice and use instead of the prawns.
Calories per serving 461

lamb stuffed with rice & peppers

Calories per serving **412**
Serves **4**
Preparation time **40 minutes**
Cooking time **1 hour
20 minutes**

2 **red peppers**, cored,
deseeded and halved
50 g (2 oz) **wild rice**, cooked
5 **garlic cloves**, chopped
5 **semi-dried tomatoes**,
chopped
2 tablespoons chopped **flat
leaf parsley**
625 g (1¼ lb) **boneless leg
of lamb**, butterflied
salt and **pepper**
4 **artichoke** halves

Put the pepper halves in a roasting tin and cook in
a preheated oven, 180°C (350°F), Gas Mark 4, for
20 minutes, until the skin has blackened and blistered.
Cover with damp kitchen paper and set aside. When the
peppers are cool enough to handle, peel off the skin
and chop the flesh. (Leave the oven on.)

Mix together one of the chopped peppers, the rice,
garlic, tomatoes and parsley. Season to taste.

Put the lamb on a board and make a horizontal incision,
almost all the way along, to make a cavity for stuffing.
Fold back the top half, spoon in the stuffing and fold
back the top. Secure with skewers.

Cook the lamb for 1 hour, basting frequently and
adding the artichokes and other pepper for the last
15 minutes of cooking time. Slice the lamb and serve
immediately with roasted new potatoes, if liked.

For lamb stuffed with coriander & mint, combine
the grated rind and juice of 1 lime, 2 finely chopped
spring onions, 2 tablespoons each chopped fresh
coriander and chopped mint, 2 tablespoons olive oil,
2 finely chopped garlic cloves, and season. Spoon over
the lamb, roll and skewer, then roast as above.
Calories per serving 379

seafood hotpot

Calories per serving **413**
Serves **4**
Preparation time **25 minutes**
Cooking time **15 minutes**

1 teaspoon **sesame oil**
1 tablespoon **vegetable oil**
3 **shallots**, chopped
3 **garlic cloves**, crushed
1 **onion**, sliced
150 ml (¼ pint) **coconut milk**
150 ml (¼ pint) **water**
3 tablespoons **rice wine vinegar**
1 **lemon grass stalk**, chopped
4 **kaffir lime leaves**
1 **red chilli**, chopped
300 ml (½ pint) **fish stock** or
  water
1 tablespoon **caster sugar**
2 **tomatoes**, quartered
4 tablespoons **fish sauce**
1 teaspoon **tomato purée**
375 g (12 oz) **straight-to-wok
  rice noodles**
375 g (12 oz) **tiger prawns**,
  heads removed and peeled
125 g (4 oz) **squid**, cleaned
  and cut into rings
175 g (6 oz) **clams**, scrubbed
400 g (13 oz) can **straw
  mushrooms**, drained
20 **basil leaves**

Heat the sesame and vegetable oils together in a large pan, add the shallots and garlic and fry gently for 2 minutes or until softened but not browned.

Add the onion, coconut milk, measurement water, vinegar, lemon grass, lime leaves, chilli, stock or water and sugar to the pan, bring to the boil and boil for 2 minutes. Reduce the heat and add the tomatoes, fish sauce and tomato purée and cook for 5 minutes. Stir in the rice noodles.

Add the prawns, squid rings, clams and mushrooms to the hotpot and simmer gently for 5–6 minutes or until the seafood is cooked. Stir in the basil leaves. Serve the hotpot immediately.

For nuoc mam dipping sauce, to serve as an accompaniment, mix the following ingredients together: 6 tablespoons fish sauce, 2 teaspoons caster sugar, 1 tablespoon rice wine vinegar, 3 finely chopped hot red chillies and 2 finely chopped hot green chillies. Leave to stand for 1 hour. **Calories per serving 25**

chicken wrapped in parma ham

Calories per serving **431**
Serves **4**
Preparation time **10 minutes**
Cooking time **10 minutes**

4 boneless, skinless **chicken breasts**, about 150 g (5 oz) each
4 slices of **Parma ham**
4 **sage leaves**
plain flour, for dusting
25 g (1 oz) **butter**
2 tablespoons **olive oil**
4 sprigs **cherry tomatoes on the vine**
150 ml (½ pint) **dry white wine**
salt and **pepper**

Lay each chicken breast between 2 sheets of clingfilm and flatten with a rolling pin or meat mallet until wafer thin. Season with salt and pepper.

Lay a slice of Parma ham on each chicken breast, followed by a sage leaf. Secure the sage and ham in position with a cocktail stick, then lightly dust both sides of the chicken with flour. Season again with salt and pepper. .

Heat the butter and oil in a large frying pan over a high heat, add the chicken and cook for 4–5 minutes on each side or until the juices run clear when pierced with a knife. Add the tomatoes and wine to the pan and bubble until the wine has thickened and reduced by about half. Serve immediately, accompanied by a green salad.

For veal escalopes with rosemary & pancetta, take 4 veal escalopes, about 150 g (5 oz) each, and flatten as above. Top each flattened escalope with a scattering of rosemary leaves, then wrap each one in a slice of pancetta, instead of the Parma ham, omitting the sage. Dust with flour, season with salt and pepper and cook as above. **Calories per serving 341**

trout with pesto

Calories per serving **422**
Serves **4**
Preparation time **10 minutes**
Cooking time **10 minutes**

4 tablespoons **olive oil**, plus
 extra for greasing
4 **trout fillets**, about 200 g
(7 oz) each
large handful of **basil**, roughly
 chopped, plus extra to
 garnish
1 **garlic clove**, crushed
50 g (2 oz) **Parmesan
 cheese**, freshly grated
salt and **pepper**
salad, to serve

Brush a baking sheet lightly with oil and place under a preheated very hot grill to heat up.

Put the trout fillets on to the hot sheet, sprinkle with salt and pepper and place under the grill for 8–10 minutes until lightly browned and the fish flakes easily when pressed with a knife.

Meanwhile, put the basil and garlic into a bowl. Work in the oil using a hand-held blender, then stir in the Parmesan cheese.

Remove the fish from the grill, transfer to serving plates, drizzle with the pesto, sprinkle with extra basil leaves to garnish and serve with salad.

For orange & almond trout, put the trout fillets on a foil-lined grill rack as above. Mix together the finely grated rind and juice of 1 small orange, 1 tablespoon chopped parsley and 4 tablespoons olive oil. Brush the mixture over the fillets and season with salt and pepper. Grill until golden and opaque, then sprinkle with toasted flaked almonds. Serve with a simple salad. **Calories per serving 403**

sesame-crusted salmon salad

Calories per serving **422**
Serves **4**
Preparation time **25 minutes**
Cooking time **4–10 minutes**

4 **spring onions**
2 **egg whites**
1 tablespoon **white sesame seeds**
1 tablespoon **black sesame seeds**
500 g (1 lb) **salmon fillet**
1 **frisée (curly-leaved endive)**, divided into leaves
2 bunches of **watercress**
salt and **pepper**

Dressing
3 tablespoons **white wine vinegar**
5 tablespoons **vegetable oil**
1 tablespoon **sesame oil**
1 tablespoon **soy sauce**
1 teaspoon **caster sugar**
1 bunch of **chives**, finely chopped

Cut the spring onions into thin strips and put them in cold water.

Lightly beat the egg whites. Mix the white and black sesame seeds with salt and pepper on a large plate. Dip the salmon fillet in the egg whites, then roll it in the sesame seeds. Pat the salmon on the seeds all over to give a good, even coating. Heat a griddle pan, add the salmon and cook for 2 minutes each side for rare or 5 minutes for well done.

Make the dressing by mixing together the vinegar, oils, soy sauce, caster sugar and chives. Toss the frisée leaves and watercress in the dressing. Arrange the leaves on a large serving dish.

Finely slice the salmon fillet and place on top of the salad. Drain the spring onion curls, dry them on kitchen paper and sprinkle over the salmon. Serve immediately.

For sashimi salmon salad, grate 1 raw beetroot and 2 carrots and mix with 100 g (3½ oz) rocket. Make the dressing as above. Mix together 1 tablespoon each white and black sesame seeds. Slice as thinly as possible 2 skinless fillets of fresh salmon, each 150 g (5 oz), and arrange on individual plates. Drizzle the dressing over the salad, garnish with the sesame seeds and serve with the salmon. **Calories per serving 338**

pepper crusted loin of venison

Calories per serving **424**
Serves **4**
Preparation time **10 minutes**
Cooking time **30–45 minutes**

750 g (1 ½ lb) **loin of venison**,
  cut from the haunch
75 g (3 oz) **mixed
  peppercorns**, crushed
2 tablespoons **juniper berries**,
  crushed
1 **egg white**, lightly beaten
salt and **pepper**

Make sure that the venison fits into your grill pan;
if necessary, cut the loin in half to fit.

Mix together the peppercorns, juniper berries and some
salt in a large, shallow dish. Dip the venison in the egg
white, then roll it in the peppercorn mixture, covering
it evenly all over.

Cook the venison under a preheated hot grill for
4 minutes on each of the four sides, turning it carefully
so that the crust stays intact. Transfer the loin to a lightly
greased roasting tin and cook in a preheated oven,
200°C (400°F), Gas Mark 6, for another 15 minutes for
rare and up to 30 minutes for well done (the time will
depend on the thickness of the loin of venison).

Leave the venison to rest for a few minutes, then slice
it thickly and serve with green beans, redcurrant jelly
and finely sliced sweet potato crisps.

For Chinese-style venison steaks with pak choi,
omit the peppercorns and juniper berries and replace
the loin of venison with four 175 g (6 oz) venison
steaks. Make a marinade by mixing together
3 tablespoons soy sauce, 1 tablespoon each finely
grated fresh root ginger, oyster sauce and rice wine,
2 crushed garlic cloves and 2 tablespoons groundnut oil.
Marinate for up to an hour, then griddle for 3–4 minutes
on each side. Serve with noodles and pak choi.
Calories per serving 429

tuna enchiladas

Calories per serving **437**
Serves **4**
Preparation time **10 minutes**
Cooking time **15 minutes**

2 ripe **tomatoes**
1 **red onion**, peeled and finely
chopped
1 tablespoon **lime juice** or
to taste
8 **chapattis**
300 g (10 oz) can **tuna in
spring water**, drained
150 g (5 oz) **reduced-fat
Cheddar cheese**, grated
salt and **pepper**
fresh coriander, chopped,
to garnish

Chop the tomatoes and mix them with the onion. Season well and add lime juice to taste.

Spoon some of the tomato mixture over each chapatti, top with the tuna and half the cheese. Roll up each chapatti and arrange them in a heatproof dish. Sprinkle over the remaining cheese and any remaining tomato salsa.

Cover and cook in a preheated oven, 200°C (400°F), Gas Mark 6, for 15 minutes until golden. Garnish with coriander and serve immediately.

For veggie enchiladas, slice and grill 12 mushrooms and 2 courgettes and and use instead of the tuna. For extra spice, add a chopped and deseeded jalapeño pepper to the tomatoes and onions. **Calories per serving 402**

chilli pork with pineapple rice

Calories per serving **440**
Serves **4**
Preparation time **20 minutes,
  plus marinating**
Cooking time **15 minutes**

2 tablespoons **sunflower oil**
2 tablespoons **lime juice**
2 **garlic cloves**, crushed
1 **red chilli**, deseeded and
  finely chopped
300 g (10 oz) **pork fillet**,
  cubed
200 g (7 oz) **Thai fragrant
  rice**
6 **spring onions**, finely sliced
200 g (7 oz) **pineapple**,
  peeled and diced
½ **red onion**, cut into wedges
1 **lime**, cut into wedges
salt and **pepper**
ready-made **sweet chilli
  sauce**, to serve

Presoak 8 wooden skewers in warm water. Mix together the oil, lime juice, garlic, chilli and salt and pepper in a bowl, add the pork and stir to coat. Cover and refrigerate for at least 1 hour.

Meanwhile, cook the rice in lightly salted boiling water for 12—15 minutes or according to the instructions on the packet. Drain and stir through the spring onions and pineapple.

Thread the pork on to the skewers, alternating it with onion and lime wedges, and cook under a preheated hot grill for about 10 minutes, turning frequently and basting with the remaining marinade, until the pork is cooked through.

Put the skewers and rice on a plate with the sweet chilli sauce and serve immediately.

For chilli gammon, replace the pork with 300 g (10 oz) cubed gammon and use 1 green pepper, cut into wedges, instead of the lime. When threading the gammon onto the skewers, alternate it with onion wedges and green pepper wedges. Serve with mango chutney instead of sweet chilli sauce. **Calories per serving 454**

beef & flat noodle soup

Calories per serving **442**
Serves **6**
Preparation time **30 minutes**
Cooking time **2 hours**

1 tablespoon **vegetable oil**
500 g (1 lb) **braising beef**
1.8 litres (3 pints) **beef stock**
4 **star anise**
1 **cinnamon stick**
1 teaspoon **black peppercorns**
4 **shallots**, thinly sliced
4 **garlic cloves**, crushed
7 cm (3 inch) piece of **fresh
   root ginger**, finely sliced
300 g (10 oz) **flat rice noodles**
125 g (4 oz) **bean sprouts**
6 **spring onions**, thinly sliced
handful of **fresh coriander**
250 g (8 oz) **beef fillet**, sliced
2 tablespoons **fish sauce**
salt and **pepper**
hot red chillies, to garnish

Nuoc cham sauce
2 **red chillies**, chopped
1 **garlic clove**, chopped
1½ tablespoons **caster sugar**
1 tablespoon **lime juice**
1 tablespoon **rice wine
   vinegar**
3 tablespoons **fish sauce**

Heat the oil in a large saucepan or casserole and sear the beef on all sides until thoroughly brown.

Add the stock, star anise, cinnamon, black peppercorns, half the shallots, the garlic and ginger. Bring to the boil, removing any scum. Reduce the heat, cover the pan with a lid and simmer very gently for about 1½ hours or until the beef is tender.

To make the nuoc cham sauce, pound the chilli, garlic and sugar until smooth, using a pestle and mortar. Add the lime juice, vinegar, fish sauce and 4 tablespoons water and blend together well.

When the beef from the broth is tender, lift it out and slice it thinly. Add the noodles to the broth and cook gently for 2–3 minutes to soften. Add the bean sprouts, along with the sliced beef and heat for 1 minute. Divide the broth, noodles and bean sprouts into warmed serving bowls. Scatter with the beef fillet, spring onions, coriander and remaining shallots. Garnish with the chillies. Serve with the nuoc cham sauce.

For tofu and flat noodle soup, replace the beef with 250 g (8 oz) tofu, cut into small squares and drained on kitchen paper. Sear as above. Replace the beef stock with the same quantity of vegetable stock and replace the fish sauce with the same quantity of soy sauce throughout. Reduce the cooking time to 20 minutes. Add 150 g (5 oz) frozen soya beans with the noodles.
Calories per serving 330

swordfish with onion & sultanas

Calories per serving 446
Serves **4**
Preparation time **10 minutes**
Cooking time **20 minutes**

4 tablespoons **olive oil**
1 **onion**, thinly sliced
1 **celery stick**, sliced
2 tablespoons **sultanas**
1 **bay leaf**
3 tablespoons **pine nuts**
2 **garlic cloves**, sliced
4 **swordfish steaks**, about
  2.5 cm (1 inch) thick
plain flour, seasoned with **salt**
  and **pepper**, for coating
150 ml (¼ pint) **dry white
  wine**

Heat half the oil in a large, heavy-based frying pan over a low heat. Add the onion, celery, sultanas and bay leaf and cook for 8–10 minutes until soft and golden. Stir in the pine nuts and garlic and cook for a further 2 minutes. Remove to a dish.

Heat the remaining oil in the pan over a high heat. Turn the swordfish steaks in the seasoned flour to coat on both sides. Add to the hot oil and cook for 3 minutes on each side until golden brown.

Return the onion mixture to the pan and pour in the wine. Boil vigorously for 2 minutes. Serve immediately.

For tuna with onion & olives, follow the first step above, but omit the sultanas and replace the pine nuts with 50 g (2 oz) halved, pitted black olives. Continue with the recipe as above, but use 4 tuna steaks, about 2.5 cm (1 inch) thick, instead of the swordfish steaks. **Calories per serving 423**

sugar & spice salmon

Calories per serving **499**
Serves **4**
Preparation time **5 minutes**
Cooking time **10 minutes**

4 **salmon fillets**, about 200 g
  (7 oz) each
3 tablespoons **light
  muscovado sugar**
2 **garlic cloves**, crushed
1½ teaspoons **cumin seeds**,
  crushed
1 teaspoon smoked or ordinary
  paprika
1 tablespoon **white wine
  vinegar**
3 tablespoons **groundnut oil**,
  plus extra for oiling
salt and **pepper**
2 **courgettes**, sliced into thin
  ribbons
lemon or **lime slices**, to serve

Put the salmon fillets in a lightly oiled roasting tin. Mix together the sugar, garlic, 1 teaspoon crushed cumin seeds, paprika, vinegar and a little salt in a bowl, then spread the mixture all over the fish so that it is thinly coated. Drizzle with 1 tablespoon of oil.

Bake in a preheated oven, 220°C (425°F), Gas Mark 7, for 10 minutes or until the fish is cooked through.

Heat the remaining oil in a large frying pan, add the remaining crushed cumin seeds and fry for 10 seconds. Add the courgette ribbons, season with salt and pepper and stir-fry for 2–3 minutes until just softened.

Transfer to warm serving plates and serve the salmon on top, garnished with lemon or lime wedges.

For salmon with pesto crust, put the salmon in a lightly oiled roasting tin, season with pepper and add a squeeze of lemon juice. Mix together 4 tablespoons pesto and 2 handfuls of fresh white breadcrumbs in a bowl, then spread on top of the salmon. Grate Parmesan cheese over the top and drizzle with olive oil. Bake as above and serve with green beans and new potatoes. **Calories per serving 483**

duck, clementine & tatsoi salad

Calories per serving **403**
Serves **4—6**
Preparation time **20 minutes**
Cooking time **15 minutes**

3 **duck breasts,** each about
225 g (7½ oz)
300 g (10 oz) **green beans,**
trimmed
3 **clementines,** peeled and
segmented
200 g (7 oz) **tatsoi** or **spinach**

Dressing
juice of 2 **clementines**
1 tablespoon **white wine**
vinegar
4 tablespoons **olive oil**
salt and **pepper**

Put the duck breasts, skin side down, in a cold ovenproof dish and cook over a medium heat for 6 minutes or until the skin has turned crisp and brown. Turn them over and cook for a further 2 minutes. Transfer the duck to a preheated oven, 180°C (350°F), Gas Mark 4, and cook for 5 minutes until cooked through. Remove the duck breasts from the oven, cover with foil and leave to rest.

Meanwhile, blanch the green beans in lightly salted boiling water for 2 minutes until cooked but still firm and bright green. Drain and refresh in cold water. Transfer the beans to a large salad bowl with the clementine segments.

Make the dressing by whisking together the clementine juice, vinegar and oil in a small bowl. Season to taste with salt and pepper.

Add the tatsoi or spinach to the beans and clementines, drizzle over the dressing and combine well. Slice the duck meat, combine it with the salad and serve immediately.

For orange & mustard dressing, an alternative dressing for this salad, cut 2 oranges in half and place them, flesh side down, on a hot griddle pan. Cook until they are charred and golden. Squeeze the orange juice into a small saucepan and reduce over a medium heat for 5 minutes until slightly thickened. Whisk in 1 tablespoon wholegrain mustard and 4 tablespoons olive oil. Allow to cool slightly and serve warm. **Calories per serving 429**

taverna-style grilled lamb with feta

Calories per serving **456**
Serves **4**
Preparation time **8 minutes**
Cooking time **6–8 minutes**

500 g (1 lb) leg or **shoulder of lamb**, diced

Marinade
2 tablespoons chopped **oregano**
1 tablespoon chopped **rosemary**
grated rind of 1 **lemon**
2 tablespoons **olive oil**
salt and **pepper**

Feta salad
200 g (7 oz) **feta cheese**, sliced
1 tablespoon chopped **oregano**
2 tablespoons chopped **parsley**
grated rind and juice of 1 **lemon**
½ small **red onion**, finely sliced
3 tablespoons **olive oil**

Mix together the marinade ingredients in a non-metallic bowl, add the lamb and mix to coat thoroughly. Thread the meat on to 4 skewers.

Arrange the sliced feta on a large serving dish and sprinkle over the herbs, lemon rind and sliced onion. Drizzle over the lemon juice and oil and season with salt and pepper.

Cook the lamb skewers under a preheated hot grill or in a griddle pan for about 6–8 minutes, turning frequently until browned and almost cooked through. Remove from heat and leave to rest for 1–2 minutes.

Serve the lamb, with any pan juices poured over, with the feta salad.

For pork with red cabbage, replace the lamb with the same quantity of lean, boneless pork. Marinate and cook the pork as above. Replace the feta with 250 g (8 oz) finely chopped red cabbage. Omit the oregano and swap the lemon for an orange. Mix the ingredients together and marinate for 5 minutes before serving.
Calories per serving 313

lime & coconut squid

Calories per serving **452**
Serves **2**
Preparation time **15 minutes**
Cooking time **5 minutes**

10–12 prepared **baby
   squid**, about 375 g (12 oz)
   including tentacles, cleaned
4 **limes**, halved

Dressing
2 **red chillies**, deseeded and
   finely chopped
finely grated rind and juice of
   2 limes
2.5 cm (1 inch) piece of **fresh
   root ginger**, peeled and
   grated
100 g (3½ oz) freshly grated
   coconut
4 tablespoons **groundnut oil**
1–2 tablespoons **chilli oil**
1 tablespoon **white wine
   vinegar**

Cut down the side of each squid so that they can be laid flat on a chopping board. Using a sharp knife, lightly score the inside flesh in a crisscross pattern.

Mix all the dressing ingredients together in a bowl. Toss the squid in half the dressing until thoroughly coated.

Heat a ridged griddle pan until smoking hot, add the limes, cut side down, and cook for 2 minutes or until well charred. Remove from the pan and set aside. Keeping the griddle pan very hot, add the squid pieces and cook for 1 minute. Turn them over and cook for a further minute or until they turn white, lose their transparency and are charred.

Transfer the squid to a chopping board and cut into strips. Drizzle with the remaining dressing and serve immediately with the charred limes and a salad of mixed green leaves.

For lemon & garlic squid, remove the tentacles from the prepared squid and slice the bodies into rings. Place in a non-metallic dish with the juice of 1 lemon and leave to marinate for 5 minutes. Heat 75 ml (3 fl oz) olive oil in a large frying pan and add 3 chopped garlic cloves and the grated rind of 1 lemon. When the oil is very hot, add the squid and cook over a high heat for 1–2 minutes or until it turns white and loses its transparency. Season with salt and pepper and serve sprinkled with parsley and with lemon wedges on the side. **Calories per serving 379**

monkfish with beans & pesto

Calories per serving **455**
Serves **4**
Preparation time **10 minutes**
Cooking time **10—15 minutes**

500 g (1 lb) **monkfish**, cut
  into 12 pieces
12 slices of **Parma ham**
12 **cherry tomatoes**
2 **yellow peppers**, cored,
  deseeded and cut into 6
  wedges
2 tablespoon **olive oil**
300 g (10 oz) can **cannellini
  beans**, rinsed and drained
4 tablespoons **ready-made
  pesto**

Presoak 4 wooden skewers in warm water. Wrap each piece of monkfish in a slice of Parma ham. Thread these on to skewers, alternating with tomatoes and pieces of yellow pepper. Brush the kebabs with the oil and cook under a preheated hot grill for 3—4 minutes. Turn the skewers over and cook for a further 3 minutes until cooked through.

Put the beans in a nonstick saucepan and cook, stirring, over low heat for 4—5 minutes or until hot. Stir in the pesto. Spoon the beans on to 4 plates, top with the kebabs and serve immediately.

For scallops with green beans & pesto, replace the monkfish with 16 scallops, wrap each one in a piece of Parma ham and skewer as above, omitting the peppers. Grill as above. Replace the cannellini beans with 250 g (8 oz) green beans and cook as above. Serve immediately, with crusty French bread on the side. **Calories per serving 375**

lamb with tangy butter beans

Calories per serving **456**
Serves **2**
Preparation time **10 minutes**
Cooking time **10 minutes**

2 tablespoons finely chopped
  mint
1 tablespoon finely chopped
  thyme
1 tablespoon finely chopped
  oregano
½ tablespoon finely chopped
  rosemary
4 teaspoons **wholegrain
  mustard**
4 **lamb cutlets**, about 125 g
  (4 oz) each

Tangy butter beans
2 teaspoons **vegetable oil**
1 **onion**, chopped
1 tablespoon **tomato purée**
50 ml (2 fl oz) **pineapple juice**
2 tablespoons **lemon juice**
a few drops of **Tabasco sauce**
250 g (8 oz) canned **butter
  beans**, drained
pepper

Mix together all the chopped herbs on a plate. Spread mustard on both sides of each noisette, then press into the herb mixture to coat evenly.

Make the tangy butter beans. Heat the oil in a frying pan, add the onion and fry gently for 5 minutes. Add the remaining ingredients to the pan and cook gently for 5 minutes.

Meanwhile, secure the thin end of the lamb around the base with a cocktail stick. Place on a foil-lined grill pan and cook under a preheated hot grill for 4 minutes on each side or until cooked but still slightly pink in the centre. Serve immediately, surrounded by the tangy butter beans.

For lamb noisettes wrapped in prosciutto, mix together 1 tablespoon finely chopped drained capers, 1 crushed garlic clove, ½ tablespoon chopped rosemary, the grated rind of ½ lemon and 1 tablespoon olive oil in a non-metallic shallow dish. Add the lamb noisettes and toss to coat in the marinade. Season well, cover and leave to marinate in the refrigerator for at least 20 minutes. Fold 4 slices of prosciutto lengthways, then wrap around the edge of each of the noisettes. Heat 1 tablespoon vegetable oil in an ovenproof frying pan and brown the prosciutto edges of the noisettes, then seal each side of the lamb briefly. Cook in a preheated oven, 200°C (400°F), Gas Mark 6, for 12–15 minutes or until cooked but still slightly pink in the centre.Remove from the oven and leave to rest before serving. **Calories per serving 395**

salmon with lime courgettes

Calories per serving **463**
Serves **4**
Preparation time **10 minutes**
Cooking time **10–15 minutes**

4 **salmon fillet** portions, about
   200 g (7 oz) each
1 tablespoon prepared
   English mustard
1.25 cm (½ inch) piece of
   fresh root ginger, peeled
   and finely grated
1 teaspoon crushed **garlic**
2 teaspoons **clear honey**
1 tablespoon **light soy sauce**
   or **tamari**
salt and **pepper**

Lime courgettes
2 tablespoons **olive oil**
500 g (1 lb) **courgettes**, thinly
   sliced lengthways
grated rind and juice of **1 lime**
2 tablespoons chopped **mint**

Lay the salmon fillet portions, skin-side down, in a shallow flameproof dish, to fit snugly in a single layer. In a small bowl, mix together the mustard, ginger, garlic, honey and soy sauce or tamari, then spoon evenly over the fillets. Season to taste with salt and pepper.

Heat the grill on the hottest setting. Cook the salmon fillets under the grill for 10–15 minutes, until lightly charred on top and cooked through.

Meanwhile, to prepare the lime courgettes, heat the oil in a large nonstick frying pan, add the courgettes and cook, stirring frequently, for 5–6 minutes or until lightly browned and tender. Stir in the lime rind and juice and mint and season to taste with salt and pepper.

Serve the salmon hot with the courgettes.

For stir-fried green beans to serve in place of the lime courgettes, cut 500 g (1 lb) green beans into 5 cm (2 inch) lengths. Heat 2 tablespoons vegetable oil in a wok or large frying pan, add 2 crushed garlic cloves, 1 teaspoon grated fresh root ginger and 2 thinly sliced shallots and stir-fry over a medium heat for 1 minute. Add the beans and ½ teaspoon salt and stir-fry over a high heat for 1 minute. Add 1 tablespoon light soy sauce and 150 ml (¼ pint) chicken or vegetable stock and bring to the boil. Reduce the heat and cook, stirring frequently, for a further 4 minutes, or until the beans are tender and the liquid has thickened. Season with pepper and serve immediately with the salmon. **Calories per serving 482**

chickpeas with chorizo

Calories per serving **461**
Serves **4**
Preparation time **10 minutes**
Cooking time **about
10 minutes**

2 tablespoons **olive oil**
1 **red onion**, finely chopped
2 **garlic cloves**, crushed
200 g (7 oz) **chorizo
sausage**, cut into 1 cm
(½ inch) dice
2 ripe **tomatoes**, deseeded
and finely chopped
3 tablespoons chopped
parsley
2 x 400 g (13 oz) cans
chickpeas, drained
salt and **pepper**

Heat the oil in a large nonstick frying pan, add the
onion, garlic and chorizo and cook over a medium-high
heat, stirring frequently, for 4–5 minutes.

Add the tomatoes, parsley and chickpeas to the pan
and cook, stirring frequently, for 4–5 minutes or until
heated through.

Season to taste with salt and pepper and serve
immediately or leave to cool to room temperature.
Serve with crusty bread, if liked.

**For harissa-spiced chickpeas with haloumi
& spinach**, heat the oil in a large saucepan, add
2 chopped onions and the garlic, omitting the chorizo,
and cook over a low heat until softened. Omit the fresh
tomatoes and parsley and add 2 tablespoons harissa
paste, the chickpeas and 2 x 400 g (13 oz) cans
chopped tomatoes to the pan. Bring to the boil, then
reduce the heat and simmer for about 5 minutes. Add
250 g (8 oz) cubed haloumi cheese and 200 g (7 oz)
baby leaf spinach and cook over a low heat for a further
5 minutes. Season to taste with salt and pepper and stir
in the juice of 1 lemon. Serve with grated Parmesan
cheese and warm crusty bread. **Calories per serving 470**

salmon & bulgar wheat pilaf

Calories per serving **478**
Serves **4**
Preparation time **10 minutes**
Cooking time **10—15 minutes**

475 g (15 oz) boneless,
  skinless **salmon**
250 g (8 oz) **bulgar wheat**
75 g (3 oz) frozen **peas**
200 g (7 oz) **runner beans**,
  chopped
2 tablespoons chopped
  chives
2 tablespoons chopped flat
  leaf **parsley**
salt and **pepper**

To serve
2 **lemons**, halved
low-fat yogurt

Cook the salmon in a steamer or microwave for about 10 minutes. Alternatively, wrap it in foil and cook in a preheated oven, 180°C (350°F), Gas Mark 4, for 15 minutes.

Meanwhile, cook the bulgar wheat according to the instructions on the packet and boil the peas and beans. Alternatively, cook the bulgar wheat, peas and beans in the steamer with the salmon.

Flake the salmon and mix it into the bulgar wheat with the peas and beans. Fold in the chives and parsley and season to taste. Serve immediately with lemon halves and yogurt.

For ham & bulgar wheat pilaf, pan-fry 300 g (10 oz) diced lean ham instead of the salmon. Replace the runner beans with the same quantity of broad beans and fold in 2 tablespoons chopped mint along with the chives and parsley. **Calories per serving 450**

teriyaki beef with rice noodles

Calories per serving **480**
Preparation time **15 minutes,
  plus marinating**
Cooking time **10 minutes**
Serves **4**

500 g (1 lb) **sirloin steak**
250 g (9 oz) **dried rice ribbon
  noodles**
2 teaspoons **sesame oil**
2.5 cm (1 inch) piece of **fresh
  root ginger**, peeled and
  finely grated
1 **garlic clove**, finely sliced
100 g (3½ oz) **mangetout**,
  sliced
1 **carrot**, cut into matchsticks
4 **spring onions**, shredded
handful of **coriander**, chopped

Teriyaki marinade
2 tablespoons **gluten-free soy
  sauce**
2 tablespoons **sake**
1 tablespoon **mirin**
½ tablespoon **caster sugar**

Make the marinade by mixing together all the ingredients in a small jug. Place the beef in a dish, pour over the marinade, cover and marinate in the refrigerator for at least 2 hours, preferably overnight.

Soak the rice noodles in boiling water according to the pack instructions. Drain well.

Preheat a griddle, meanwhile, so it is really hot. Place the beef on the griddle, reserving the marinade, and cook for 2–3 minutes on each side. Transfer to a chopping board and leave to rest.

Heat the oil in wok or large frying pan, add the ginger and garlic and fry for 30 seconds. Add the vegetables and cook until just beginning to soften.

Add the coriander, noodles and 2–3 tablespoons of the marinade and heat through. Spoon on to 4 serving plates, slice the beef and serve on top of the noodles.

For Thai beef salad, mix together the marinade ingredients as above, adding 1 teaspoon sesame oil, the grated rind and juice of 1 lime, 3 tablespoons Thai fish sauce, a handful each of chopped coriander, mint and Thai basil. Cover and chill. When ready to serve, griddle the beef as above. Using a peeler, slice ½ cucumber and 2 carrots into ribbons and stir into the chilled dressing with 4 shredded spring onions, 12 halved cherry tomatoes and 200 g (7 oz) salad leaves. Slice the steak thinly, stir into the salad and serve. **Calories per serving 296**

trout with cucumber relish

Calories per serving **424**
Serves **4**
Preparation time **10 minutes**
Cooking time **10–12 minutes**

4 **rainbow trout**, cleaned and
  gutted
1 tablespoon **sesame oil**
crushed **Szechuan pepper**,
  to taste
salt
chopped **chives**, to garnish
lemon wedges, to serve

For the cucumber relish
1 **cucumber**, about 20 cm
  (8 inches) long
2 teaspoons **salt**
4 tablespoons **rice vinegar**
3 tablespoons **caster sugar**
1 **red chilli**, deseeded and
  sliced
3 cm (1¼ inch) piece **fresh
  root ginger**, peeled and
  grated
4 tablespoons **cold water**

Make the cucumber relish. Cut the cucumber in half lengthways, scoop out and discard the seeds and cut the flesh into 1 cm (½ inch) slices. Put in a glass or ceramic bowl. In a small bowl, put the salt, vinegar, sugar, chilli and ginger, add the water and mix well. Pour over the cucumber, cover and leave to marinate at room temperature while you cook the trout.

Brush the trout with the oil and season to taste with crushed Szechuan pepper and salt. Place the trout in a single layer on a grill rack and grill for 5–6 minutes on each side or until cooked through. Leave to rest for a few moments, then garnish with chopped chives and serve with the cucumber relish and lemon wedges.

For trout with chestnut dressing, brush the trout with 1 teaspoon olive oil and season to taste with salt and black pepper. While the trout is cooking as above, put 100 g (3½ oz) peeled chestnuts in a small saucepan over a medium heat and cook, stirring constantly, until lightly browned. Remove from the heat, add 4 tablespoons olive oil, 3 tablespoons lemon juice and 2 tablespoons chopped parsley, and season to taste with salt and pepper. Stir well, then return to the heat for 2 minutes. Pour the dressing over the cooked trout, garnish with parsley sprigs and serve immediately. **Calories per serving 499**

salmon & puy lentils with parsley

Calories per serving **486**
Serves **4**
Preparation time **15 minutes**
Cooking time **35 minutes**

200 g (7 oz) **Puy lentils**
1 **bay leaf**
200 g (7 oz) fine **green beans**,
 chopped
25 g (1 oz) **flat leaf parsley**,
 chopped
2 tablespoons **Dijon mustard**
2 tablespoons **capers**, rinsed
 and chopped
2 tablespoons **olive oil**
2 **lemons**, finely sliced
about 500 g (1 lb) **salmon
 fillets**
1 **fennel bulb**, finely sliced
salt and **pepper**
dill sprigs, to garnish

Put the lentils into a saucepan with the bay leaf and enough cold water to cover (do not add salt). Bring to the boil, reduce to a simmer and cook for 30 minutes or until tender. Season to taste, add the beans and simmer for 1 minute. Drain the lentils and stir in the parsley, mustard, capers and oil. Discard the bay leaf.

Meanwhile, arrange the lemon slices on a foil-lined grill pan and put the salmon and fennel slices on top. Season the salmon and fennel and cook under a preheated hot grill for about 10 minutes or until the salmon is cooked through.

Serve the fennel slices and lentils with the salmon on top, garnished with dill sprigs.

For pork escalopes with lentils, prepare the Puy lentils as above and replace the salmon with 4 pork escalopes. Grill the pork as above, omitting the fennel. Meanwhile, finely slice 2 celery sticks and toss with a little walnut oil. Serve the lentils with the escalopes on top, garnished with the celery and walnut oil.
Calories per serving 437

beef in red wine

Calories per serving **490**
**(not including potatoes or
polenta)**
Serves **4**
Preparation time **10 minutes**
Cooking time **2¼ hours**

875 g (1¾ lb) **brisket of beef**,
cut into 5 cm (2 inch) pieces
1 **celery stick**, sliced
2 **bay leaves**
750 ml (1¼ pint) bottle **Barolo**
or other full-bodied **red wine**
300 ml (½ pint) **beef** or
chicken stock
2 **carrots**, cut at an angle into
3.5 cm (1½ inch) slices
20 **baby onions**, peeled but
kept whole
salt and **pepper**

Season the beef with salt and pepper and put in
a large, flameproof casserole with a tight-fitting lid.
Add the celery and bay leaves, then pour in the wine
and stock. Bring to the boil, then reduce the heat to a
barely visible simmer and cook, covered, for 1½ hours,
stirring occasionally.

Add the carrots and onions. Re-cover and simmer
gently for a further 45 minutes, adding a little water
if the sauce becomes too thick.

Remove the beef from the heat and serve with mashed
potatoes or soft polenta, if liked.

For oxtail in red wine with tomatoes, replace the
beef with 2 kg (4 lb) oxtail chunks. Cook as above,
adding a 400 g (13 oz) can chopped tomatoes and
reducing the red wine to 350 ml (12 fl oz). Simmer
gently for 2½ hours. Oxtail releases a lot of fat, so
ideally make the stew a day ahead, leave to cool
completely, then refrigerate. Skim off all the solidified
layer of fat before reheating. **Calories per serving 463**

mussels with cider

Calories per serving **490 (not including French bread)**
Serves **2**
Preparation time **10 minutes**
Cooking time **9 minutes**

1.5 kg (3 lb) small **farmed mussels**
2 **garlic cloves**, chopped
150 ml (¼ pint) **dry cider**
100 g (3½ oz) **double cream**
2 tablespoons chopped **parsley**
salt and **black pepper**

Wash the mussels thoroughly, discarding any that do not close when tapped and put in a large saucepan with the garlic and cider. Bring to the boil, cover and cook over a medium heat for 4–5 minutes until all the shells have opened. Discard any that remain closed after cooking.

Strain the mussels through a colander and put in a large bowl, cover with foil and place in a very low oven to keep warm.

Pass the cooking juices through a fine sieve into a clean saucepan and bring to the boil. Whisk in the cream and simmer for 3–4 minutes, or until thickened slightly. Season to taste with salt and pepper.

Pour the sauce over the mussels, scatter over the parsley and serve immediately with plenty of crusty French bread to mop up the juices, if liked.

For mussels with Asian flavours, wash the mussels thoroughly, discarding any that do not close when tapped and put in a large saucepan with 2 sliced garlic cloves, 2 teaspoons grated fresh root ginger, 4 sliced spring onions and 1 sliced red chilli. Add a splash of water and cook as above. Strain the mussels and keep warm. Strain the cooking juices through a fine sieve into a clean saucepan. Whisk in 100 g (3½ oz) coconut cream and heat through. Pour over the mussels and served garnished with chopped fresh coriander. **Calories per serving 314**

butterbean & chorizo stew

Calories per serving **470**
Preparation time **10 minutes**
Cooking time **20 minutes**
Serves **4**

1 tablespoon **olive oil**
1 large **onion**, chopped
2 **garlic cloves**, crushed
200 g (7 oz) **chorizo
  sausage**, sliced
1 **green pepper**, cored,
  deseeded and chopped
1 **red pepper**, cored,
  deseeded and chopped
1 glass **red wine**
2 x 400 g (13 oz) cans
  butterbeans, drained
  and rinsed
400 g (13 oz) can **cherry
  tomatoes**
1 tablespoon **tomato purée**
salt and **black pepper**
chopped **parsley**, to garnish
gluten-free crusty bread,
  to serve

Heat the oil in a flameproof casserole, add the onion and garlic and fry for 1–2 minutes. Stir in the chorizo and fry until beginning to brown. Add the peppers and fry for 3 minutes.

Pour in the wine and allow to bubble, then stir in the butterbeans, tomatoes and tomato purée and season well. Cover and simmer for 15 minutes. Ladle into shallow bowls, sprinkle with the parsley to garnish and serve with crusty bread, if liked.

For garlic prawns with butterbeans, cook the onion and garlic as above, then stir in 300 g (10 oz) raw peeled and deveined tiger prawns instead of the chorizo and fry until they just turn pink. Add the butterbeans, 3 tablespoons light crème fraîche and 2 handfuls of rocket leaves and season well. Heat through and serve. Calories per serving 243

griddled tuna salad

Calories per serving **451**
Serves **4**
Preparation time **10 minutes**
Cooking time **15 minutes**

500 g (1 lb) small **new
  potatoes**, scrubbed
4 fresh **tuna steaks**, about
  175 g (6 oz) each
100 g (3½ oz) **baby spinach
  leaves**, roughly chopped
4 tablespoons **olive oil**
2 tablespoons **balsamic
  vinegar**
salt and **pepper**
griddled **lime wedges**,
  to serve

Place the new potatoes in a steamer over boiling water
and cook for 15 minutes or until tender.

Meanwhile, heat a griddle pan. Pat the tuna fillets dry
with kitchen paper and cook in the pan for 3 minutes on
each side for rare, 5 minutes for medium or 8 minutes
for well done.

Remove the potatoes from the steamer. Slice them in
half and place in a bowl. Add the spinach, olive oil and
balsamic vinegar. Toss and season to taste. Divide the
salad between 4 plates and serve with a slice of tuna
arranged on the top of each, and a griddled lime wedge
for squeezing.

For warm niçoise salad, cook the potatoes and tuna
as above. Halve and blanch 125 g (4 oz) fine beans
and quickly fry 125 g (4 oz) cherry tomatoes. Add the
beans and tomatoes and 125 g (4 oz) black olives to
the halved warm potatoes and spinach leaves. Flake
the tuna and add to the salad. Season well and serve.
Calories per serving 496

prawn, pea shoot & quinoa salad

Calories per serving **492**
Serves **4**
Preparation time **10 minutes**
Cooking time **10 minutes**

300 g (10 oz) **quinoa**
75 g (3 oz) **mangetout**,
  blanched and halved
200 g (7 oz) **asparagus
  spears**, cooked, cooled and
  cut into bite-sized pieces
50 g (2 oz) **pea shoots**
400 g (13 oz) cooked **tiger
  prawns**, shells removed
salt and **pepper**

Fruit and nut dressing
2 tablespoons **olive oil**
2 tablespoons **lemon juice**
20 g (¾ oz) **dried cranberries**
50 g (2 oz) **hazelnuts**,
  chopped and toasted

Cook the quinoa according to the instructions on the packet. Set aside to cool.

Stir the mangetout and asparagus through the quinoa.

Make the dressing by mixing together the oil, lemon juice, cranberries and hazelnuts.

Spoon the pea shoots and prawns over the quinoa, drizzle over the dressing and serve.

For prawn, bulgar wheat & nut salad, use 300 g (10 oz) bulgar wheat instead of the quinoa. For a nuttier dressing, toast 50 g (2 oz) flaked almonds in a dry pan with the hazelnuts, then mix with the olive oil and the rind and juice of 1 orange. **Calories per serving 485**

quick prosciutto & rocket pizza

Calories per serving **498**
Serves **4**
Preparation time **10 minutes**
Cooking time **10 minutes**

4 mini **pizza bases**
2 **garlic cloves**, halved
250 g (8 oz) **reduced-fat
mozzarella cheese**,
shredded
8 **cherry tomatoes**, quartered
150 g (5 oz) **prosciutto**, sliced
50 g (2 oz) **rocket leaves**,
washed
balsamic vinegar, to taste
salt and **pepper**

Rub the top surfaces of the pizza bases with the cut faces of the garlic cloves.

Put the pizza bases on a baking sheet, top with mozzarella and tomatoes and bake in a preheated oven, 200°C (400°F), Gas Mark 6, for 10 minutes until the bread is golden.

Top the pizzas with slices of prosciutto and rocket leaves, season to taste with salt, pepper and balsamic vinegar and serve immediately.

For tuna & pineapple pizza, drain and chop a 220 g (7½ oz) can pineapple, and drain and flake a 160 g (5½ oz) can tuna in spring water. Top the pizza bases with the pineapple and tuna, then scatter over the mozzarella and tomatoes before cooking as above. **Calories per serving 481**

blackened salmon with salsa

Calories per serving **496**
Serves **4**
Preparation time **15 minutes**
Cooking time **8 minutes**

3 tablespoons **Cajun
  seasoning**
1 teaspoon **dried oregano**
4 **salmon fillets**, about 75 g
  (3 oz) each
sunflower oil, to brush
lime wedges, to garnish

Cajun salsa
410 g (13½ oz) can **black-
  eyed beans**, rinsed and
  drained
2 tablespoons **olive oil**
1 **avocado**, peeled, stoned
  and chopped
2 **plum tomatoes**, finely
  chopped
1 **yellow pepper**, deseeded
  and finely chopped
2 tablespoons **lime juice**
salt and **pepper**

Mix together the Cajun seasoning and oregano in a
shallow bowl.

Brush the salmon on both sides with a little oil and
coat with the spice mix, making sure the fish is
completely covered. Set aside.

Meanwhile, make the salsa by mixing together all the
ingredients in a bowl. Season to taste and set aside.

Cook the salmon in a preheated, dry frying pan for
4 minutes on each side.

Slice the salmon and serve with the salsa, with lime
wedges to garnish.

For salsa verde, drain and finely chop 6 anchovy fillets
in oil and combine them with 3 tablespoons chopped
basil, 3 tablespoons chopped parsley or chives,
2 teaspoons roughly chopped capers, 2 teaspoons Dijon
mustard, 3 tablespoons olive oil and 1½ tablespoons
white wine vinegar. **Calories per serving 335**

cambodian fish pot

Calories per serving **499**
Serves **4**
Preparation time **10 minutes**
Cooking time **15 minutes**

1 teaspoon **sesame oil**
1 tablespoon **vegetable oil**
3 **shallots**, chopped
3 **garlic cloves**, crushed
1 **onion**, halved and sliced
600 ml (1 pint) canned **coconut milk**
3 tablespoons **rice wine vinegar**
1 **lemon grass stalk**, chopped
4 **kaffir lime leaves**
3–6 **red bird's eye chillies**, halved and seeds removed
300 ml (½ pint) **fish stock**
1 tablespoon **caster sugar**
2 **tomatoes**, quartered
2 tablespoons **fish sauce**
1 teaspoon **tomato purée**
175 g (6 oz) **live clams**, cleaned
375 g (12 oz) raw peeled **tiger prawns**
125 g (4 oz) **squid**, cleaned and cut into rings
400 g (13 oz) can **straw mushrooms**, drained
20 **holy basil leaves** (optional)

Heat the sesame and vegetable oils together in a large flameproof casserole, add the shallots and garlic and fry gently for 2 minutes or until softened but not browned.

Add the onion, coconut milk, rice wine vinegar, lemon grass, lime leaves, chillies, stock and sugar to the casserole and bring to the boil. Boil for 2 minutes, then reduce the heat and add the tomatoes, fish sauce and tomato purée and cook for 5 minutes.

Discard any clams that don't shut when tapped, then add them with the prawns, squid rings and mushrooms to the casserole and simmer gently for 5–6 minutes or until the prawns turn pink, the squid are cooked through and the clams have opened. Discard any clams that remain closed. Stir in the basil leaves, if liked.

Serve the hotpot immediately with rice noodles.

For traditional fisherman's stew, replace the sesame and vegetable oils with olive oil and fry the garlic and shallots as above. When adding the onion, replace the coconut milk, rice wine vinegar, lemon grass, lime leaves, chillies, stock and sugar with 2 x 400 g (13 oz) cans chopped tomatoes, 1 pinch saffron threads, 300 ml (½ pint) white wine and 600 g (1¼ lb) white fish fillets, skinned and cut into bite-sized chunks. Continue as above, adding the tomatoes, fish sauce and tomato purée, then the prawns, squid rings, and mushrooms, but replace the basil leaves with chopped parsley. Serve with crusty bread instead of the noodles, dipping sauce and fresh coriander. **Calories per serving 393**

roast pork with fennel

Calories per serving **451**
Serves **4**
Preparation time **10 minutes**
Cooking time **30 minutes**

625 g (1 ¼ lb) **pork fillet**
1 large **rosemary sprig**, broken into short lengths, plus extra sprigs to garnish
3 **garlic cloves**, peeled and sliced
4 tablespoons **olive oil**
1 large **fennel bulb**, trimmed and cut into wedges, central core removed
1 large **red onion**, cut into wedges
1 large **red pepper**, halved, deseeded and cut into chunks
150 ml (¼ pint) **white wine**
75 g (3 oz) **mascarpone cheese** (optional)
salt and **pepper**

Pierce the pork with a sharp knife and insert the pieces of rosemary and garlic evenly all over the fillet. Heat half the oil in a roasting tin on the hob, add the pork and cook for 5 minutes or until browned all over.

Add the fennel, onion and red pepper to the roasting tin and drizzle the vegetables with the remaining oil. Season well with salt and pepper. Roast in a preheated oven, 230°C (450°F), Gas Mark 8, for 20 minutes or until the juices run clear when the pork is pierced in the centre with a knife.

Transfer the pork and vegetables to a serving plate and keep hot in the oven. Add the wine to the roasting tin and simmer on the hob until slightly reduced. Stir in the mascarpone, if using.

Cut the pork into slices and arrange on serving plates with spoonfuls of the roasted vegetables and a spoonful or two of the sauce. Serve immediately garnished with rosemary sprigs.

For roast pork with apples & cider sauce, pierce the pork, flavour with rosemary and fry as above. Thickly slice 6 apples with assorted colour skins. Heat 2 teaspoons butter and 1 tablespoon olive oil in a large frying pan and fry the onion, red pepper and apples for 4–5 minutes over a moderately high heat until golden and soft. Transfer to a roasting tin, arrange the pork on top and roast as above. Keep the meat and vegetables warm. Make the sauce as above with 150 ml (¼ pint) cider instead of wine and reduce before stirring in the mascarpone and 1 teaspoon Dijon mustard. Season to taste and serve as above. **Calories per serving 499**

index

acknowledgements

Commissioning editor: Eleanor Maxfield
Senior editor: Elinor Smith
Art direction and design: Eoghan O'Brian
Production controller: Allison Gonsalves

All photos © Octopus Publishing Group

Stephen Conroy 11, 18, 23, 31, 53, 75, 79, 107, 110, 113,
141, 143, 155, 159, 169, 179, 193, 195, 199, 201, 205,
209, 215, 219, 233; Will Heap 15, 25, 41, 59, 61, 81, 93,
101, 133, 147, 181, 235; William Lingwood 29, 69, 203;
David Loftus 177, 191; Neil Mersh 207; David Munns 163;
Sean Myers 225; Lis Parsons 1, 2, 5, 6, 9, 12, 16, 33, 45, 65,
83, 91, 95, 97, 103, 115, 123, 127, 129, 137, 149, 151, 157,
161, 165, 173, 175, 187, 189, 197, 211, 217, 227, 229,
231; William Reavell 21, 37, 49, 125; Gareth Sambidge 63,
73, 117, 185; William Shaw 14, 39, 43, 47, 51, 77, 85, 89,
99, 105, 109, 121, 135, 145, 153, 213, 223; Eleanor Skan
67, 87; Simon Smith 13, 27, 57; Ian Wallace 8, 10, 35, 55,
71, 119, 131, 139, 171, 221; Philip Webb 183